OSPREY
PUBLISHING

Nelson's Sailors

D1519085

Gregory Fremont-Barnes · Illustrated by Steve Noon

First published in Great Britain in 2005 by Osprey Publishing,
Midland House, West Way, Botley, Oxford OX2 0PH, UK
443 Park Avenue South, New York, NY 10016, USA
E-mail: info@ospreypublishing.com

© 2005 Osprey Publishing Ltd.

A CIP catalogue record for this book is available from the British Library

ISBN 1 84176 906 1

Design: Ken Vail Graphic Design, Cambridge, UK
Index by David Worthington
Originated by The Electronic Page Company, Cwmbran, UK
Printed in China through World Print Ltd.

05 06 07 08 09   10 9 8 7 6 5 4 3 2 1

FOR A CATALOGUE OF ALL BOOKS PUBLISHED BY OSPREY MILITARY AND
AVIATION PLEASE CONTACT:

NORTH AMERICA
Osprey Direct, 2427 Bond Street, University Park, IL 60466, USA
E-mail: info@ospreydirectusa.com

ALL OTHER REGIONS
Osprey Direct UK, P.O. Box 140 Wellingborough, Northants, NN8 2FA, UK
E-mail: info@ospreydirect.co.uk

www.ospreypublishing.com

Artist's note

Readers may care to note that the original paintings from
which the colour plates in this book were prepared are
available for private sale. All reproduction copyright
whatsoever is retained by the Publishers. All enquiries
should be addressed to:

Steve Noon
50 Colchester Avenue
Penylan
Cardiff
CF23 9BP
UK

The Publishers regret that they can enter into no
correspondence upon this matter.

CONTENTS

NELSON'S SAILORS

INTRODUCTION

'A vessel of war contains a little community of human beings, isolated, for the time being, from the rest of mankind. This community is governed by laws peculiar to itself; it is arranged and divided in a manner suitable to its circumstances.' So observed Samuel Leech in his memoirs of life as an ordinary seaman in Nelson's navy.

'Jack', as contemporaries termed the common British sailor, who inhabited the microcosm that Leech knew intimately, was a paradoxical character. Illiterate, coarse and prone to all manner of immorality, he was also nearly always unfailingly generous, good-natured and industrious. He was the product of a society that professed a vague attachment to the concept of liberty, and yet, by today's standards, placed ex-cessive constraints on its application and expression. The British sailor was noted for the loyalty shown to his shipmates, not to mention to his sovereign and nation. With rare exceptions he accepted, albeit grudgingly, the uncompromising authority of his superiors aboard the vessel that constituted his home over many years of triumph and tragedy. He rarely questioned his harsh environment. He was, after all, the product of an age in which poverty, sickness and death were a painful and pervasive reality and in which society defined and punished criminality much more harshly than it does today.

The popular image of the British sailor of the French Revolutionary and Napoleonic Wars (1793–1815) is of a press-ganged wretch living off weevil-infested, rotting food, motivated only by prize money, compelled to endure years of boredom and back-breaking work, and facing constant hazards aboard a floating hell, his conduct carefully scrutinized by his officers and discipline maintained with the lash. This is not wholly untrue, but it is a narrow view of a much wider picture.

'Son of the ocean.' A fine example of a seaman in his best shore-going outfit, complete with smart jacket, waistcoat, neck scarf, and buckles to his hat and shoes. (Philip Haythornthwaite)

CHRONOLOGY

1793 Britain, with the Royal Navy as her principal weapon, joins other European powers in opposing French expansion on the Continent and at sea (February).

1794 Battle of the Glorious First of June, the first Anglo-French fleet action of the war.

1796 Spain, possessing a substantial navy, allies herself with France and declares war on Britain.

1797 Channel fleet at Spithead mutinies (April). North Sea fleet at the Nore follows suit in May. Government concedes major concessions over sailors' living conditions and rates of pay. Admiral Duncan defeats a Dutch squadron at Camperdown (October).

1798 Battle of the Nile (August). Nelson isolates and destroys the French Mediterranean fleet, thereby isolating Bonaparte and his army in Egypt.

1801 Battle of Copenhagen (April). Nelson defeats the Danish fleet at anchor.

1802 Peace of Amiens brings short-lived end to the French Revolutionary Wars (March).

1803 War resumes between Britain and France, ushering in the Napoleonic Wars (May).

1804 Spain declares war against Britain, again adding her navy to the balance of power at sea (December).

1805 Battle of Trafalgar (October). Nelson decisively defeats the Franco-Spanish fleet, so foiling any future French attempts to invade Britain.

1812 Angered by the impressment of its sailors by the Royal Navy and hoping to annex Canada, the United States declares war on Britain, thereby expanding the scope of Britain's naval commitments (June).

1815 Final defeat of Napoleon at Waterloo brings the Napoleonic Wars to a close (June). Anglo-American conflict also concludes (February).

Pitt and Napoleon carving up the globe. With France holding virtual mastery over continental Europe, Britain, for the sake of her own survival, maintained control of the seas. (Royal Naval Museum)

RECRUITMENT, RATING AND PAY

Volunteers

With the nation's defence entirely dependent on the strength and readiness of the Royal Navy, the needs of the service were insatiable. While each year Parliament voted money for what easily constituted the nation's largest employer, the navy never mustered full strength. In 1805, for instance, the navy stood at 109,000 – a substantial number in its own right and the largest in the world at the time, but still considered insufficient at a time when the nation faced imminent invasion from Napoleonic France.

Each captain had the responsibility of gathering enough men for his ship: ordinary seamen did not belong to the navy, but rather to a particular vessel. This the captain might achieve by posting handbills in port cities, indicating a rendezvous and waiting for men to appear for enlistment. The payment of a bounty to every man who enlisted played an important part in a captain's armoury, and many volunteered for precisely this reason. In 1797, the navy offered £70, or five years' wages for an ordinary seaman – a substantial sum at a time when the state provided no security to those without work and, even in the world's most prosperous nation, grinding poverty was commonplace.

Men and boys were, in fact, motivated by many factors – adventure, escape from poverty, the lure of the bounty or prize money, escape from family ties, avoidance of prison, or a combination of these. William Robinson summed up the attraction felt by many young men who naively viewed the naval service in its most optimistic light:

> To the youth possessing anything of a roving disposition it is attractive. Nay, it is seducing … When steadily pursued and with success, it enables the mind, and the seaman feels himself a man … No profession can vie with it, and a British seaman has a right to be proud, for he is incomparable when placed alongside those of any other nation. Great Britain can truly boast of her hearts of oak, the floating sinews of her existence, and the high station she holds in the political world.

Twelve-year-old Samuel Leech was enticed by the visit of his cousin, 'A smart, active sailor, over six feet in height and well proportioned … He was so jolly, so liberal, and so full of pleasant stories, that I began to feel quite sure that sailors were noble fellows.' But the

Able seaman. A ship's surgeon noted that men like this 'could undergo the fatigues and perils of sea life; there seems a necessity for being inured to it from an early age. The mind, by custom and example, is thus trained to brave the fury of the elements in their different forms, with a degree of contempt at danger and death that is to be met with nowhere else, and which has become proverbial.' (National Maritime Museum)

realities of life at sea were well known to contemporaries, and some of Leech's relatives sought to dampen his ardour.

He was not deterred. Leech left his quiet Oxfordshire village in July 1810.

> Henceforth my lot was to be cast amid noise, dissipation, storms and danger. This, however, disturbed my mind but little; brushing away a tear, I leaped gaily on to the outside of the coach, and in a few minutes, enveloped in a cloud of dust, was on my way to London, filled with the one absorbing idea, 'I am going to sea! I am going to sea!'

William Robinson was also keen to join the navy, enlisting at the naval recruiting centre at Tower Hill, in London, in May 1805. He soon regretted his foolhardy decision and

> began to repent of the rash step I had taken, but it was of no avail, submission to the events of fate was my only alternative, murmuring or remonstrating, I soon found, would be folly. After having been examined by the doctor, and reported *seaworthy*, I was ordered down the hold, where I remained all night with my companions in wretchedness, and the rats running over us in numbers ... Upon getting on board this vessel, we were ordered down in the hold, and the gratings put over us; as well as a guard of marines placed round the hatchway, with their muskets loaded and fixed bayonets, as though we had been culprits of the first degree, or capital convicts.
>
> In this place we spent the day and the following night huddled together, for there was not room to sit or stand separate: indeed, we were in a pitiable plight, for numbers of them were sea-sick, some retching, others were smoking, whilst many were so overcome by the stench, that they fainted for want of air.

Once aboard his appointed ship a new recruit was required to take the oath of allegiance, promising to serve the king faithfully, and his name was officially entered into the ship's books. If he could not write his name, as was very often the case, he simply signed with an 'X'. In return, he received a certificate signed by an admiral, which identified him by his name as well as by his physical description, including age, height, hair and eye colour, and any distinguishing features, such as a tattoo or scar, to make the

Sailor and sweetheart. With his ship due to sail, he must make his painful farewells. (Philip Haythornthwaite)

Sailor's return. A young sailor arrives at his poverty-stricken home bearing prize money. Captured vessels were 'bought' by the Admiralty and the value of the prize distributed among the officers and men. Ordinary seamen only received one-eighth of the total value between them, but even this could amount to several years' wages. (Philip Haythornthwaite)

transfer of the certificate to another man more difficult. The sailor then received his bounty and was taken to the purser to be issued with clothing.

Impressment

Notwithstanding Britain's fine naval traditions, the Admiralty never reached the quota of men it required. With appalling food and hygiene, harsh discipline, low pay and inadequate services, the lure of the sea held little appeal. These realities, combined with the fact that both Parliament and the public hypocritically viewed conscription as an infringement of liberty, obliged the navy to return to the notorious system of 'impressment', or forced recruitment, once the needs of the navy could not be met by other means. Impressment, whose origins lay in medieval times, was commonly practised in this period, particularly in seaports. Though it ceased to be resorted to after 1815, it was not legally

abolished until 1833, and its widespread practice established the common misconception that the Royal Navy's lower ranks consisted almost exclusively of pressed men.

From the start of the wars in 1793 all seamen, fishermen, watermen and mariners generally – that is, those working on the rivers – aged 18 to 55 were subject to being pressed, unless their specialist trade (for example, whalers) or their position (such as mates in merchant ships) offered them exemption, or if they were Sea Fencibles (part-time soldiers, liable for service at home or in home waters, for defence against invasion) and were therefore already performing a vital service for the country. In order to avoid being pressed, such men had to have protections that described themselves, issued by the Admiralty. However, a 'press from protections' could be enforced, negating the force of this document. Finally, gentlemen, or at least those who appeared to be so by their manner of dress, were also exempt, and landsmen were

A press gang operating on Tower Green, London. The figure on the right appears to be a local tavern keeper awaiting payment for the information he provided on the whereabouts of suitable candidates for abduction. (National Maritime Museum)

generally avoided as largely useless aboard ship. In reality, however, a determined press gang, encouraged by financial incentives (the leader of a gang would receive at least £1 for every man apprehended), might take men and boys with no previous experience of the sea. While regulations directed gangs to avoid taking landsmen, some inevitably were taken and found themselves in His Majesty's service very much against their will. The whim of a captain sometimes played its part in the type of men sought. Robinson relates how his captain went so far as to stop a merchantman solely for the purpose of impressing its two best musicians 'for the captain's amusement', rather than to increase the size of the ship's company, already at full complement.

The Impress Service, a permanent body formalized in 1793, maintained gangs in 51 ports in Britain and Ireland, organized into 32 districts each commanded by a regulating naval captain, who received an additional £5 a month for his troubles. He established a rendezvous for the gang, often an inn, with a press room, so situated that men seized could not be rescued. A press gang was usually led by a lieutenant, who bore a warrant signed by the Lords of the Admiralty, and about ten men. With this authority the press gang could seize men ashore or afloat, except from outward-bound ships. From inward-bound ships, any men pressed had to be compensated for by 'men in lieu', which meant providing the vessel with experienced navy men who would assist in sailing the ship home, after which they rejoined their own vessel. In practice, ships were plundered of their best men, whoever they were, and the men left in lieu were often of poor quality whose return was not required. Merchant ships in the open sea were particularly vulnerable, as were privateers, whose entire crews could be taken. Where avoidance of the 'press' appeared impossible, such men could 'volunteer', thus qualifying for the bounty,

a phenomenon that renders impossible a precise calculation of exactly how many men were pressed in this period.

Pressed men were brought, by force if necessary, to a press tender, a small vessel moored in the vicinity, and led by another lieutenant, and then to the receiving ship, perhaps a hulk moored in the royal dockyards or along the coast, such as at Gravesend, Great Yarmouth, Liverpool and Bristol. Outside of England, these could also be found in Ireland, and in Bombay, Malta and Jamaica. Taken to the hold, impressed men were guarded by marines, and held sometimes for weeks, before finally joining their appointed ships. In the meantime, many would suffer and sometimes succumb to diseases, especially typhus.

Escape from impressment could be achieved legitimately, or through bribery or subterfuge. It was possible to fend off a press gang by the legally recognized means of a ticket of leave, which granted a sailor time on shore with his captain's consent. The exemption of gentlemen resulted in various ruses being tried. One sailor disguised himself, borrowing from a custom house officer, at the cost of half a guinea, a gilt-headed cane, powdered wig, cocked hat and long coat. 'I got a waterman to put me on shore,' the seaman recounted.

I am confident my own father, had he been alive, could not have known me … I inquired of the waterman the way to the inn where the coach set out for London … All those precautions were necessary. Had the waterman suspected me to be a sailor, he would have informed the press gang in one minute. The waiters at the inn would have done the same.

Even if a man were unfortunate enough to find himself in the custody of a press gang, he might still go free, for a captain sometimes

Press gangs at work in a port town. (Philip Haythornthwaite)

released some of his quarry as unfit for service. As pressed men were necessarily a mixed lot, captains were not always satisfied with them, describing some in their letters as 'blackguards', 'sad thievish creatures', 'a nuisance to the ship', 'ragged and half dead' and 'sad wretches'. By and large, however, if a man were reasonably sound in mind and body, however ignorant he might be of the sea, he could still be employed in various ways around the ship where brawn, not brains, was the overriding requirement.

One thing, however, was clear: once aboard ship a man faced little prospect of release until hostilities ceased. In the meantime, all the freedoms hitherto enjoyed on land evaporated. 'Whatever may be said about this boasted land of liberty', Robinson explained,

> whenever a youth resorts to a receiving ship for shelter and hospitality, he, from that moment, must take leave of the liberty to *speak*, or to act; he may *think*, but he must confine his thoughts to the *hold* of his mind, and never suffer them to escape the *hatchway* of utterance.

Rating

Every man aboard a ship was assigned a rate by the first lieutenant, recorded in the muster book. A man's pay and duties were defined by his 'rating', which was subject to change at the whim of the captain, who could promote or disrate a seaman whenever he chose. Similarly, when a seaman was transferred to another ship the new first lieutenant could reassign his rate. In ascending order, the system of rates began with boy (or volunteer) third and second class, for boys under 15, and 15 to 17 – these being usually officers' servants (as well as naval apprentices) and seamen in training – respectively. Above this was the rate of landsman, for those who had no experience of the sea at all, and who performed such uncomplicated tasks as hoisting and lowering sails, rigging tackle and swabbing the decks. These men were followed by ordinary seamen, who understood the rigging but were less experienced or simply incompetent. Finally, there were able seamen, who could perform tasks such as reefing and steering, and generally possessed a decent standard of seamanship. They could potentially rise to the status of petty or warrant officer.

Those men aspiring to promotion could look to one of over 20 petty officer rates, of which there were three classes, formally designated in 1808 for the purposes of dividing prize money. The cook and the master-at-arms were petty officers holding warrants from the Navy Board, but subject to disrating for failing to do their duty. The most junior of the petty officers were such men as the quarter gunners, cooper, trumpeter and others. Above them were the captains of the tops, afterguard and other positions on the ship, and the mates of the master specialists. Above these, and most senior, were such master specialists as sailmaker, caulker and ropemaker, the quartermaster, coxswains, the master-at-arms (who served as the ship's policeman), and the midshipman. Only in very rare cases did an ordinary seaman ever rise to receive an officer's commission.

Pay

A seaman was not technically enlisted in the navy, but assigned to a specific ship and, although he could be transferred from one vessel to another without his consent, he received no pay while his name did not appear on a particular ship's books. Pay was low and provided only on an irregular basis. When the wars with France began in 1793 the monthly rates of pay for the lowest ranks were as follows: able seaman £1 4s; ordinary seaman 19s; landsman 19s. As a result of the pay rise agreed in the wake of the great mutinies in 1797, an able seaman received £1 9s 6d; an ordinary seaman £1 3s 6d; and a landsman £1 2s 6d. In 1806 slight increases were made to the two higher ranks, while pay to landsmen remained unchanged.

Robinson described a typical pay day:

> There is not perhaps one in twenty who actually knows what he is going to receive, nor does the particular amount seem to be a matter of much concern; for, when paid, they hurry down to their respective berths, redeem their honour with their several ladies and bomb-boat men [carrying goods and prostitutes to the ships in harbour], and then they turn their thoughts to the Jew pedlars …

Once discharged from service, a sailor was paid all arrears in full. One Jack Ellis, after release in 1814 from five years' imprisonment in France, received all his back pay and prize money owed him from operations since the time of his capture.

SHIPBOARD ORGANIZATION, ROUTINE AND DUTIES

Ships were crowded places, ranging from a complement of 841 officers and men for a first rate (a ship of the line carrying 100 guns or more), to 250–280 officers and men for a 44-gun frigate, 160 officers and men for a 22-gun sixth-rate vessel, and proportionally smaller numbers for brigs and gunboats. Managing this number of men occupying a confined space required a careful system of organization and division of labour.

Watches

A ship was a world unto itself, with every man responsible for specified functions. As Leech explained,

> when its members first come together, each one is assigned his respective station and duty. For every task, from getting up the anchor to unbending the sails, aloft and below, at the mess-tub or in the hammock, each task has its man, and each man his place. A ship contains a set of *human* machinery, in which every man is a wheel, a band, or a crank, all moving with wonderful regularity and precision to the *will* of its machinist – the all-powerful captain.

In order to perform the various tasks required to operate a ship of war, the crew was divided into two or three watches. Some of the men were 'idlers', such as the carpenter, the cook, sailmaker and boatswain, who being employed throughout the day were not required to keep night-watch and therefore kept no watch, though most of them had to work on deck when the captain summoned 'all hands'. Watches were divided into groups, each man assigned a task according to his abilities. Thus there was a group to work each mast, and one for the forecastle, waist and quarterdeck (the afterguard).

Watches were divided in the following manner:

Noon–4pm	Afternoon watch
4pm–6pm	First dogwatch
6pm–8pm	Second dogwatch
8pm–midnight	First watch
Midnight–4am	Middle watch
4am–8am	Morning watch
8am–noon	Forenoon watch

The first lieutenant divided the ship's company, that is, the men, boys and marines (but not the idlers) into two or three watches, each subdivided into divisions, which were commanded by a lieutenant and midshipman, who looked after the men's welfare. If the ship operated on a three-watch system, then each watch could sleep through two nights in three. The two-watch system was the more common and a safer one, for by it half the ship's company was on duty at one time, while the other rested below, though the disadvantage was obvious: neither watch

Sailor furling a topsail. Such tasks required strength, agility and bravery in the face of high winds and rolling seas. (National Maritime Museum)

slept more than four hours at a time. If two watches were used, they were called the larboard watch and starboard watch. If there were three, the third was known as the middle watch. Every member of a watch was expected to remember his assigned position in the ship for each of his duties (e.g. working in the rigging, crewing a gun, etc.), and another for those occasions when both watches were called.

Watches were timed according to a four-hour sand glass that sat at the door of the captain's cabin and was guarded by the marine sentry normally appointed to stand there; there was also a separate glass that measured a half hour. When it emptied, the midshipman of the watch turned it over and the sentry rang the bell, once for the first half hour and twice for the second. In this fashion the time was known by bells, for example five bells meant two and a half hours, and eight bells meant four hours, or the end of the watch. The men did not serve the same watch each day.

Morning watch
Between 6 and 8am the watch below decks was awakened. With the pipe of 'Up all hammocks ahoy!', Leech explained,

Seaman catting the anchor of a ship of the line, *c.*1815. Catting involved raising and securing the anchor to the side of the ship or onto the deck. (National Maritime Museum)

> signs of life make their appearance. Rough, uncouth forms are seem tumbling out of their hammocks on all sides, and before its last sounds have died upon the air, the whole company of sleepers are hurriedly preparing for the duties of the day. No delay is permitted, for as soon as the … officers have uttered their imperative commands, they run below, each armed with a rope's-end, with which they belabour the shoulders of any luckless wight upon whose eyes sleep yet hangs heavily, or whose slow-moving limbs show him to be but half awake.

The men rolled up their hammocks and stowed them in the hammock nettings along the sides of the upper deck and the poop. At eight bells the men were piped to breakfast, the cook and his mates having lit the galley fires soon after the middle watch. This left only the lookouts, helmsman and officer of the watch on deck. In most ships the hands had half an hour (one glass) for breakfast, which usually consisted of oatmeal gruel, and constituted the first food they had had since 4pm the previous day. According to this timetable, only the idlers (who possessed specialist skills) had had more than four hours' continuous sleep. 'By this regular system of duty', Robinson explains, 'I became inured to the roughness and hardships of a sailor's life.'

One of the principal duties of the morning watch was to wash and scrub the weather deck with holystones, so named because they were approximately the size of a prayer book, before rubbing them dry. The men pulled off their shoes and stockings, rolled up their trousers above their knees and pushed the holystones along the planks. Robinson described how 'the men suffer from being obliged to kneel down on the wetted deck, and a gravelly sort of sand strewed over it. To perform this work they kneel with their bare knees, rubbing the deck with a stone and the sand, the grit of which is often very injurious.'

Forenoon watch

While the watch on deck performed their various tasks, the watch below cleaned the lower deck with holystones and then moved on to other jobs such as working on the masts or yards, exercising the guns or practising with small arms, or with the boats, sometimes in tandem with the watch on deck. The idlers were also at work by this time. Men in the hold had by this time brought up the allotment of food for the day to the steward's room, from which the mess cooks carried it in mess kids (large bowls with rope handles) to their respective messes (see below) or to the galley. If the captain had ordered punishment to be administered that day, the men were piped at six bells to witness it being carried out. Lookouts were posted at the fore and main mastheads and on deck throughout the day, relieved on an hourly basis.

Afternoon watch

Dinner, the main meal of the day, was served during this watch, when the boatswain's mate piped the men to assemble in their respective messes where the mess cook would bring it from the galley in mess kids. Captains usually allowed an hour for eating, sometimes longer. When one bell was sounded, a tune was played as a signal for the mess cooks to come to the scuttlebutt by the mainmast, where a petty officer or other man of a similar rating, in the company of a watchful officer, mixed the grog (diluted rum). Once the meal was concluded, those hands who had been working were allowed time to themselves.

First and second dogwatches

During these watches, supper was piped and the second half of the day's grog distributed. The men had as much as an hour to consume their food and drink, usually followed by time for exercise on the great guns with live ammunition. At the end of the first dogwatch, the watches changed. At the end of the second dogwatch, hammocks were hung up and the watch on deck and the idlers retired to sleep, extinguishing all the lights and fires before they did so. As fire was an innate danger on a ship, the master-at-arms and his corporals walked along the decks to ensure that this vital procedure was uniformly carried out.

First watch and middle watch

These watches fell during the evening, when there were usually at least six lookouts on the deck, all of whom would call out 'all's well' to the officer of the watch every time a glass was turned. Unless the ship needed to be tacked or worn round, or required a sail to be taken in, the watch on deck had nothing arduous to do, thus enabling some captains to allow the men to sleep on deck. Meanwhile, the watch below continued to sleep until the middle watch was piped, unless of course 'all hands on deck' was called.

Whatever the duty to be performed, alacrity was demanded in every instance. As Leech explained,

> rapidity attends the performance of every duty. The word of command is given in the same manner, and its prompt obedience enforced by the ... unceremonious rope's-end.

Messes

In each watch the boys and men divided themselves into messes of between four and 12 each for eating and drinking. In larger vessels the men could be organized again, into divisions, and without regard to watches – one assigned to each lieutenant, assisted by a midshipman or master's mate to look after a section of it. By these means the men could be monitored for the sake of their cleanliness and health.

Once a month seamen could apply to change messes, and Leech did precisely that:

> The mess to which I was introduced was composed of your genuine, weather-beaten, old tars. But for one of its members, it would have suited me very well; this one, a real gruff old 'bull-dog,' named Hudson, took [it] into his head to hate me at first sight. He treated me with so much abuse and unkindness,

Sailors at their mess. Note the mess kid on the table and ditty bags suspended from the beams. With space at a valuable premium, everything was stowed to maximize access to the guns. Despite its complex appearance, a ship was, in the end, little more than a floating platform for cannon. (National Maritime Museum)

that my messmates soon advised me to change my mess, a privilege which is wisely allowed, and which tends very much to the good fellowship of a ship's crew; for if there are disagreeable men among them, they can in this way be got rid of; it is no unfrequent case to find a few, who have been spurned from all the messes in the ship, obliged to mess by themselves.

Having changed messes, Leech found he fitted in fairly well:

The jocularity, pleasantry, humour and good feeling that now prevailed on board our frigate, somewhat softened the unpleasantness of my lot, and cultivated a feeling of reconciliation to my circumstances. Various little friendships, which sprang up between me and my shipmates, threw a gleam of gladness across my path; a habit of attention, respect and obedience in a short time secured me universal good will. I began to be tolerably satisfied.

Each mess was assigned a particular place in the ship, and its members kept their personal possessions and equipment there. The former were kept in ditty bags either suspended from the beams or stored in sea chests. Tables were slung from the beams and stowed when not being used, together with a bench on either side. Wooden plates and bowls were stored at the sides of the ship in racks, together with mess kids.

In contrast to the officers, who slept on cots slung from the beams and berthed in cabins, the men slept in hammocks that swung from the beams. Regulations allocated 14 inches per man while slung in a hammock, but as one watch was always on deck (provided it was a two- rather than three-watch system in use), each man actually had twice as much space. Hammocks were slung fore-and-aft, by an arrangement reached by the boatswain and the first lieutenant. Each man knew his place according to the numbered peg that identified the position of his

hammock, which was invariably near his station in case of need. Most men had two hammocks, one in which he slept and the other waiting to be cleaned on Saturdays. Hammocks were 6ft by 3ft, made of cloth, and usually holding some sort of makeshift mattress made of wool or rags, as well as a blanket and coverlet. The hammocks were the property of the Navy Board and were issued by the boatswain, but the men were expected either to provide their own bedding or buy it from the purser.

Heating below decks was provided by movable iron stoves, and fresh air was provided by sails so rigged as to direct air down the hatchways. At night the lower and middle decks (if it were a line of battle ship as opposed to a single-decked frigate or smaller vessel) were completely dark, as no lights were permitted for risk of fire. Even during the day, if the ports were closed, life below decks was largely spent in a dimly lit, smelly and dank environment. This was made all the more unpleasant since a ship was an exceedingly crowded place, and most pictures of scenes below decks exaggerate the height between decks. In many places a sailor had to lean forward or crouch to avoiding knocking his head.

A sailor wishing to relieve himself used the head, which consisted of little more than planks with a hole and a pipe that led to the sea. There were also urinals in the waist of the ship. A sailor could also simply hang from the lee channels (where the shrouds attach to the sides of the ship) and do his business directly into the water.

The ship's week
The routine of a ship depended on the discretion of the captain and navy tradition. Some reserved certain days for training in gunnery and seamanship, for washing, and for cleaning the ship. In other cases the days were divided into the same routines. Punishments might be held on

Sailors at their mess table, confined to the space between the guns. All paraphernalia, including table, benches, utensils and plates, were stowed away when not in use. Every consideration was made for the fighting efficiency of the ship, and virtually none for the comfort of the crew. (National Maritime Museum) a particular day, say once a week, or, less frequently, every day. Time was allotted for the men to make, mend or decorate their clothes, such as the fastening of ribbons in their hats or sewing them into the seams of their shirts or trousers. Foretopmen, in particular, liked to look particularly smart, as did the captain's boat crew, who were sometimes supplied with their own outfits by the captain. The men usually washed their clothes on a particular day, though they did this without soap or fresh water, which was far too precious to be used in this manner. The following day the clothes were dried and made ready for the captain's inspection.

Church services were held on Sundays, the day on which hammocks were piped up and breakfast served half an hour earlier than usual. The boatswain ensured that the men at the breakfast table were clean and ready for the muster at five bells. Having stowed their ditty bags containing their personal possessions in a particular place on the quarterdeck, they assembled, clean and shaved, by divisions for inspection on the forward part of the quarterdeck and on the gangways and forecastle, first by the midshipmen and lieutenant responsible for them, and then by the officers. The captain then inspected each division in turn. Anyone looking unkempt or otherwise poorly turned-out had their names passed to the master-at-arms who would arrange punishment at a later time. The captain then proceeded below to inspect the mess decks, galley, sickbay, storerooms and hold, instructing the first lieutenant to put right anything found out of order.

After inspection, church service commenced, with a special pennant raised at the peak. The captain and his officers assembled on the quarterdeck while the men stood in the waist, so that only the helmsman and lookouts remained on duty. If no chaplain was aboard, the captain could perform the service. Leech observed, however, that

> The Sabbath was also a day of sensuality. True, we sometimes had the semblance of religious services, when the men were

Prayers after the battle of the Nile (1798). The chaplain of HMS *Gloucester* despaired that his 'constant efforts to rebuke the seamen, etc, for profane swearing and intemperate language of every kind' proved utterly ineffective. (Royal Naval Museum)

summoned aft to hear the captain read the morning service from the church prayer-book; but usually it was observed more as a day of revelry than of worship.

If sailors were not in the habit of praying, they certainly did when their lives stood at risk, such as in a storm or during battle. 'It is strange,' Leech went on, 'that sailors who see so much peril, should treat religion with such neglect as it is usual for them to do. When danger is imminent, they send up a cry for help; when it is past, they rarely return a grateful thank-offering.'

By noon the service was over, after which dinner was served, usually to include a special dish. Apart from those aboard ships with particularly strict captains, the men were allowed to spend Sunday afternoon as they pleased, unless the weather or the presence of an enemy made this impossible.

Duties and dangers

Seamen in the rigging, or 'topmen', had to keep ropes and lines in order, and the sails furled or unfurled as orders required. These functions required great agility and fitness – indeed, something akin to the skills of an acrobat – as these men had to get about almost like monkeys, with great speed and yet with considerable care, lest they fall with dreadful consequences. Such men could run aloft along yards to yardarms even when the weather was foul. Crosswinds, rain and a rolling ship sometimes claimed a life, but the men generally adapted to this exacting task.

Forecastle men were expected to keep that part of the vessel clean and well painted, and looked after the anchor, bowsprit and fore yard. Men of the afterguard, indifferent seamen and landsmen, were responsible for braces, the spanker, main sail and lower stay-sails. In

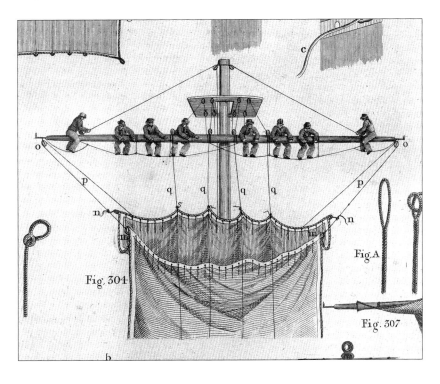

Sailors aloft. Working in the rigging proved highly dangerous, particularly in bad weather, yet many sailors took pride in their nimbleness and could carry out their functions with remarkable stoicism despite the risk of falling to almost certain death onto the deck or into the sea. (Royal Naval Museum)

HMS *Triton*, a small sixth-rate vessel of 28 guns. It was essential that part of a ship's company understood the complexities of their vessel's standing and running rigging, sails, masts and many other features. (National Maritime Museum)

action they stood at the guns on the gun deck or were issued with small arms. 'Waisters', who made up the largest proportion of the ship's company, performed various functions, including keeping the deck clean, looking after the animals, working the pumps and other menial tasks. The idlers lived in the hold. They fed and slaughtered the animals, mainly chickens, geese and pigs, made and repaired clothes and sails, repaired and coiled rope, polished brass fittings, worked as barbers, maintained the gun room, cooked, and performed many other specialized functions.

Considerable knowledge was required to understand the correct use of the combination and multiplicity of sails, both square and fore-and-aft, to be deployed in order to make the best use of the wind. Sailors not only had to understand the function of braces, tacks, bowlines and sheets; they were expected not to make mistakes, for the wind was unforgiving and a sail furled or lowered or set aback improperly could result in a broken spar or a tear in a sail. This was bad enough in the open sea, but in the midst of battle it could have serious consequences.

The danger of storms was ever-present. Robinson recalled how, during blockade duty off Rochefort, his and the other ships of the squadron

> were separated by a tremendous gale of wind, which lasted for several days … we were completely at the mercy of each succeeding mountainous wave, for we were not able to show a stitch of canvas; in this perilous situation we were, when [suddenly] the *Mars*, a 74-gun ship, appeared on the top wave, while our ship was in the valley beneath, and it was thought by all on board, that we must inevitably come into contact, strike each other, and go down.

Though his own ship survived, the *Pickle* schooner, off Quiberon Bay, lost the entire watch on deck, carried away by an enormous wave breaking over her.

Leech recalled an occasion when his ship ran into a storm in the Bay of Biscay:

> It seemed as if old Neptune really intended that wave to sink us to Davy Jones' locker. As the water rolled from side to side within, and the rude waves without beat against her, our good ship trembled from stem to stern, and seemed like a human being gasping for breath in a struggle with death.

Men who found themselves in the sea if their ship sank were generally doomed: swimming was a rare skill at this time and one, in any event, discouraged by captains, who feared men might use it to desert. Apart from clinging to wreckage there was little else a man in the water could do for survival.

Sailors working aloft climbed the shrouds, enabling them to go as far as a platform known as a top, which could be entered either by climbing over the outside edge using the futtock shrouds, or through the gap in its centre known as the 'lubber's hole'. To ascend even further the sailor used a second set of shrouds. Once he was at the desired height, he would move along the yard using the 'horse', or footrope, for his feet while grasping the yard and sail with his hands and clenching the yard under his arms. If the horses (the ropes running through the stirrups beneath the yards) were not moused (knotted with spun yarn), they could break when the first man attempted to pass across them, possibly causing him to fall on someone on the next yard below, or on someone on deck.

Even in calm conditions, working aloft offered a host of dangers, and in heavy weather the topmen literally risked their lives when performing routine tasks, even going so far as to place bets on the performance of feats of daring such as running along the yards instead of shifting carefully along them, or descending rapidly down the stays rather than clambering down the ratlines. Sometimes tragedy resulted, as happened aboard the *Macedonian* one Sunday afternoon. While reefing the topsails, one man was knocked from the yard. Leech recorded that, in falling, the seaman 'struck some part of the ship, and the wave which opened to receive him never disclosed his form again'.

Reefing was among the most difficult and strenuous duties, the more so since it was performed as the weather grew worse. It involved the hauling down of sails not needed and required a row of men to array themselves along the yard, all standing on the horse except the one at the end on the weather side. A good deal of leaning and pulling was required to perform this function and a man was liable to fall off if he were not cautious or nimble.

The lifting of objects of considerable size also posed some dangers. Many tasks aboard a warship involved shifting, raising and lowering of heavy and cumbersome objects, such as masts, yards, cannon, ships' boats, water casks and wet sails. The most common medical complaint was, not surprisingly, hernia.

Going down in a storm. Ships were remarkably resilient, and a skilled crew, taking suitable precautions, could usually ride out a storm or squall. The crew could throw cargo and guns overboard in order to avoid being driven against the rocks on a lee shore. Sails were normally reduced and in extreme circumstances the masts could be cut down to reduce top weight. (Royal Naval Museum)

FOOD AND DRINK

Food

Food for the men was provided by the Victualling Board, which ran its own breweries, bakeries and slaughterhouses, and sometimes by private contractors. Each mess sent its mess cook, usually changed each week, to collect the mess's food from the steward and bring it to the mess or to the galley if it required cooking. He would then return from the galley, having placed the food in a mess kid, and distribute it. Men used wooden utensils, bowls and plates, the latter being square (from which the expression a 'square meal' is derived). The mess cook was also responsible for collecting the grog and cleaning up after each meal. In return he received an extra measure of grog, called the 'overplus'.

Food at sea was basic, repetitive, poor at best and revolting at worst. Still, it provided sufficient calories for a man of whom a great deal of physical labour was required, and exceeded those consumed by poor men on land, who probably did not have a hot meal every day and at least four portions of meat a week. Indeed, contemporary accounts seldom refer to sailors going hungry.

The weekly allowance of food for one man was as follows:

Breakfast was served at 8am and sometimes consisted of skillygalee, a sort of oatmeal gruel prepared in fatty water and which by the time of Trafalgar included butter and sugar. Robinson records that breakfast 'usually consists of burgoo, made of coarse oatmeal and water; others will have Scotch coffee, which is burnt bread boiled in some water, and sweetened with sugar'. The men might also receive tea or cocoa –

	Bread (lb)	Beer (gals)	Beef (lb)	Pork (lb)	Pease (1/2pt)
Sun	1	1		1	1
Mon	1	1			
Tues	1	1	2		
Wed	1	1			1
Thurs	1	1		1	1
Fri	1	1			1
Sat	1	1	2		

	Oatmeal (pt)	Butter (oz)	Cheese (oz)
Sun			
Mon	1	2	4
Tues			
Wed	1	2	4
Thurs			
Fri	1	2	4
Sat			

sweetened with brown sugar – a bit of cheese, and ship's biscuit, or hard tack, made from wholemeal flour, salt and water. Ship's biscuit was often infested with weevils, so many that the men sometimes ate their biscuits at night so that the vermin could not be seen, or tapped their hard tack against the table to dislodge these pests.

Dinner was given out at noon, and always included a pint of grog at half past the hour. Robinson noted how, at the appointed time, 'the fifer is called to play *Nancy Dawson* or some other lively tune, a well known signal that the grog is ready to be served out'.

This meal could include any combination of cheese, boiled beef or pork, dried peas, duff (dough made from flour, sugar, water and pork fat, boiled in a cloth bag), with ship's biscuit. On Sundays the men might receive a treat like figgy-dowdy, made up of ship's biscuit, pork fat, plums, figs, rum and currants baked together.

Supper was served at 4pm, and also included a pint of grog. The men were issued with the usual ship's biscuit, together with heavily salted beef or pork, which was preserved in casks for up to two years, rendering it well preserved but almost inedible. It was dark and very hard – so hard, in fact, that the men could carve objects out of it and polish them. Meat was soaked for 24 hours before being boiled, together with the vegetables and the duff (in bags) in copper pots. During this process the meat produced a foamy sludge that floated on the top of the liquid. Half of this fat, or slush, was used aboard ship for greasing the rigging and the remaining half was retained by the cook, who sold it to candlemakers. He was prohibited from selling it to the crew, for it could cause scurvy, but some cooks did so secretly.

Ship's cook, a position often filled by a seaman who had been disabled in battle or otherwise injured, thus enabling him to continue in some form of employment aboard ship. (National Maritime Museum)

25

One day a week flour and suet were issued instead of meat, the former made into duff by the mess cook. Generous captains might occasionally issue a double portion of pudding, or deny this treat altogether as a punishment. 'Pease' comprised virtually the only vegetable, though sometimes the ship carried sauerkraut, which being pickled could be stored for a lengthy period.

Fresh meat was also available for limited periods at sea, for on a long cruise a ship would carry a large number of livestock, such as bullocks, pigs, sheep, goats, geese, ducks, turkeys and chickens. John Nichol refers to some of these being retained as pets, but by and large the men were not sentimental about the animals on board.

In port fresh vegetables and fruit could be obtained, these varying depending on the part of the world visited. Leech recalled that while his ship lay at Lisbon, the crew 'was well supplied with fruits from the shore. Large bunches of delicious grapes, abundance of sweet oranges, water-melons, chestnuts, and also a bountiful supply of gigantic onions, of peculiar flavour, enabled our crew to gratify their palates in true English style.'

Butter and cheese generally did not survive long aboard ship, and for ships sailing for foreign waters the usual complement was three months' supply of these precious commodities.

After these went bad the ship relied on olive oil, to the equivalent of 1pt for 1lb of butter or 2lb of cheese. Butter that went rancid was used to grease the rigging, while bad cheese had no use and was thrown overboard.

The men themselves used their own means to supplement their diets. Apart from acquiring local produce, sailors could sometimes fish if the captain permitted it, and occasionally would pool their money and buy livestock. If given liberty while in harbour, they could buy food ashore; if confined to the ship, they could purchase it from bomb-boats that crowded around the ships to sell their wares, or hope their captain would buy fish from a fishing boat. Robinson records that off Cadiz,

we sometimes fired at, and brought to, some of the Spanish fishing-boats, and by these means, a fresh meal for the crew was often obtained; for they not only had fish on board, but some would have grapes, whilst others would have fowls and eggs; and our captain was always anxious to get fresh provision for the ship's company.

Out at sea, the variation of food was considerable: dolphins, porpoises, sharks, or seabirds such as boobies, albatrosses or gulls, were all edible, though not necessarily palatable. In the Pacific, tortoises or turtles might be had, with the added advantage that these exotic beasts could be stored on the deck upside down and kept alive for several weeks.

Drink

No more essential article existed for a sailor than drink. The navy issued him with a gallon of beer every day, a staggering rate of consumption that amounted to ten times the annual national average for civilians. The Victualling Board maintained its own breweries, but when a ship was overseas it purchased beer from contractors. Beer did not keep aboard ship for very long and was therefore drunk mostly in port or in home waters, and during the early part of a long journey. It was considered safer than water, which was stored in barrels for months at a time.

Once the supply of beer was exhausted, the men received other forms of alcohol according to a formula that equated 1gal of beer with 1pt of wine or ½pt of spirits. Both wine and spirits were served diluted with water, the men certainly preferring the stronger of the two. Wine, generally red, and called 'black strap' by the men, usually came from Spain, except when conflict with that country stopped supply. White wine was known as 'Miss Taylor'.

Grog was also extremely popular. Its name derived from Admiral Vernon, who in 1740, while on the Jamaica station, issued local rum instead of brandy, but diluted it by one part rum to four parts water, and then mixed in lemon juice and brown sugar, so combating scurvy and drunkenness simultaneously. As Vernon wore a waterproof grogram boat-cloak, the men styled him 'Old Grogram', and the nickname, shortened, was applied to the drink he invented. By the time of the French Revolutionary Wars the dilution had been altered, thereby rendering the drink stronger, consisting of one part rum to three parts water, together with ½oz of lemon juice and ½oz of brown sugar. Men were not allowed to hoard or trade their alcohol, and any not drunk immediately had to be poured out. But, as the mess cook's portion was usually 2pt, known as the overplus, he did not necessarily consume it himself. Thus 'the cook can take upon himself to be a man of consequence', Robinson explains, 'for he has the opportunity of inviting a friend to partake of a glass, or of paying any little debt he may have contracted … it is grog which pays debts, and not money, in a man of war'.

Drunkenness was a perennial problem among seamen, but given the conditions and the monotony of service it is hardly surprising that a sailor should turn to this form of escape. Leech echoed the observations of so many of his contemporaries:

> One of the greatest enemies to order and happiness in ships of war is drunkenness. To be drunk is considered by almost every sailor as the *acme* of sensual bliss; while many fancy that swearing and drinking are necessary accomplishments in a genuine man-of-war's-man … Were it not for the moral and physical ruin which follows its use, one might laugh at the various contrivances adopted to elude the vigilance of officers in their efforts to procure rum …

Drunkenness was, however, occasionally tolerated. Leech recalled that at Christmas

> our ship presented a scene such as I had never imagined. The men were permitted to have their 'full swing.' Drunkenness ruled

Flogging. The entire ship's company assembled for this ritualized punishment. Marines are assembled on the poop to ensure order, while the condemned man, lashed to a grating, awaits the boatswain's mate. In the centre, another sailor appears to be confessing to the crime, attempting to spare his innocent shipmate. (Royal Naval Museum)

the ship. Nearly every man, with most of the officers, were in a state of beastly intoxication at night. Here, some were fighting, but were so insensibly drunk, they hardly knew whether they struck the guns or their opponents; yonder, a party were singing libidinous or bacchanalian songs, while all were laughing, cursing, swearing or hallooing; confusion reigned in glorious triumph; it was the very chaos of humanity.

DISCIPLINE AND PUNISHMENTS

Law in the Royal Navy was governed by the 34 Articles of War, which dated from the mid-18th century and had undergone a number of revisions before 1793. They listed various transgressions and established the punishments to be administered by a court martial, if the crime was serious enough to warrant one. The Admiralty required every captain to read the Articles to his ship's company once a month (although the captain, at his own discretion, sometimes read them on Sundays), especially since the vast majority of ordinary seamen were illiterate. They applied whether Britain was at war or peace, and whether the men were aboard ship or on land. More than half the Articles listed offences that carried the death penalty, though a court martial was not obliged to apply it in all cases.

The captain's rule aboard ship was practically absolute, and most maintained order according to strict principles of good conduct and hard work. Midshipman George Jackson, aboard the 36-gun *Trent*, recalled that 'No sailor was allowed to walk from one place to another on deck, and woe betide the unfortunate fellow who halted in his run aloft, unless expressly bidden to do so for some particular purpose.' For transgressions, the captain could administer punishment in various ways. Indeed, one Article, by its vagueness, sanctioned just about any method: 'All measures not capital shall be punished according to the customs and manners used at sea.' Robinson rightly observed that this article 'shelters the captains in the navy in resorting to almost any mode of punishment they may think proper'. Some punishments were relatively trifling, such as a verbal warning, the stopping of a man's grog or the dilution of his grog, a spell in chains below decks, or a period of time working at the pumps – a particularly arduous and loathsome task.

Seamen accepted discipline and subordination – and the attendant punishments meted out for infractions – as a matter of course. What they resented was arbitrary, draconian rule by cruel officers, especially that practised by those of the most junior rank – the midshipmen. Robinson noted one in particular with

> a wickedly mischievous disposition, whose sole delight was to insult the feelings of the seamen, and furnish pretexts to get them punished … He was a youth not more than twelve or thirteen years of age. I have often seen him get on the carriage of a gun, call a man to him, and kick him about the thighs and body, and with his fist would beat him about the head; and these, although prime seamen, at the same time dared not murmur.

The boatswain's mate and midshipmen carried a length of rope called a 'starter' with which he would strike, or 'start', those whom he regarded as slow or lazy. This punishment was often applied, but anything more serious had to be administered on the captain's order. Indeed, 'starting' was used so frequently that there was no requirement for the man administering it to log a record of the incident in the ship's books.

In a harsh age, where a man could face long imprisonment or even death for what today would be classed as misdemeanours, a ship's captain had at his disposal a dreadful array of punishments with which to enforce order and discipline aboard his vessel.

Flogging
Flogging remains the best-known form of punishment. Up to 1806 a man was liable to no more than a dozen lashes for any one offence, but a captain inclined to administer more could simply punish an offender by convicting him of more than one offence on the same occasion. Robinson observed the iniquity of the whole business:

> ... the prisoner may plead, but, in nineteen cases out of twenty, he is flogged for the most trifling offence or neglect, such as not hearing the watch called at night, not doing any thing properly on deck or aloft, which he might happen to be sent to do, when, perhaps he has been doing the best he could, and at the same time ignorant of having done wrong, until he is pounced on, and put in irons.

Punishments of a serious nature such as flogging were reserved for a particular day, when the entire crew assembled at a specified time in the afternoon when the captain ordered, 'All hands aft to witness punishment.' The marines stood guard on the poop deck overlooking the men, while the officers and midshipmen, in their best uniforms, stood on the quarterdeck.

If, upon questioning the officer of the offender's division, the captain returned a guilty verdict, the master-at-arms had the man lashed by his wrists and knees to a grating stood upright, his back exposed. 'The boatswain's mates, whose office it is to flog on board a man of war', Leech wrote,

> stood ready with their dreadful weapon of punishment, the cat-o'-nine-tails. This instrument of torture was composed of nine cords, a quarter of an inch round and about two feet long, the ends whipt with fine twine. To these cords was affixed a stock, two feet in length, covering with red baize. The reader may be sure that it is a most formidable instrument in the hands of a strong, skilful man.

Leech, continued, describing the process in grisly terms:

> The boatswain's mate is ready, with coat off and whip in hand. The captain gives the word. Carefully spreading the cords with the fingers of his left hand, the executioner throws the cat over his right shoulder; it is brought down upon the now uncovered herculean shoulders of the MAN. His flesh creeps – it reddens as if blushing at the indignity; the sufferer groans; lash follows lash, until the first mate, wearied with the cruel employment, gives place to a second. Now two dozen of these dreadful lashes have been inflicted: the lacerated back looks inhuman; it resembles roasted meat burnt nearly black before a scorching fire; … Vain are the cries and prayers of the wretched man.

The flogging ceased either when the specified number had been administered, or when the ship's surgeon intervened and declared the offender's life in danger. The remaining lashes were administered as soon as the offender had recovered sufficiently to bear them on another occasion.

Running the gauntlet

Running the gauntlet, abolished in 1806, involved a man stripped to the waist and running between two rows of men who lashed out at him with a length of rope or cord as he passed.

Gagging

Anyone who talked back to an officer was liable to this punishment, which Robinson explained thus:

> The man is placed in a sitting position, with both legs put in irons, and his hands secured behind him; his mouth is then forced open, and an iron bolt put across, well secured behind his head. A sentinel is placed over him with his drawn bayonet, and in this situation he remains, until the captain may think proper to release him, or until he is nearly exhausted.

Seamen in irons await flogging for drunkenness, c.1812. Faced with an isolating, arduous and hazardous life, sailors invariably took solace in drink, notwithstanding the risk of punishment that often followed. (National Maritime Museum)

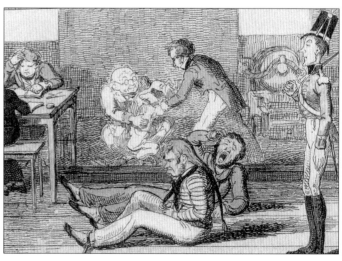

Flogging through the fleet

Apart from a death sentence, the most severe punishment in the navy was flogging through the fleet. After four impressed seamen had made an abortive attempt to desert, Robinson recalled in his memoirs,

> They were tried by a court martial [at Spithead] and sentenced to receive three hundred lashes each through the fleet ... The man is placed in a launch, *i.e.* the largest ships' boat, under the care of the master-at-arms and a doctor. Then a capstan bar is rigged fore and aft, to which the poor fellow is lashed by his wrists and, for fear of hurting him – humane creatures – there is a stocking put over each, to prevent him from tearing the flesh off in his agonies. When all is ready, the prisoner is stripped and seized to the capstan bar. Punishment commences by the officer, after reading the sentence of the court martial, ordering the boatswains' mates to do their duty. The cat-of-nine tails is applied to the bare back, and at about every six lashes a fresh boatswain's mate is ordered to relieve the executioner of his duty, until the prisoner has received, perhaps, twenty-five lashes: he is then cast loose, and allowed to sit down with a blanket rolled round him and is conveyed to the next ship, escorted by this vast number of armed boats, accompanied by the doleful music, 'the *rogues' march.*'

Hanging

The most serious crimes carried a mandatory sentence of death. These included helping or communicating with an enemy, mutiny, sedition, murder, sodomy (whether man or animal), failure to pursue an enemy and failure to fight. A sentence of death meant the condemned man was hauled up from the cathead with a bag over his head and hanged from the fore yardarm.

DESERTION AND MUTINY

Desertion

Given the harsh conditions of life aboard a warship, particularly the draconian punishments inflicted, desertion was commonplace. One estimate put the number of desertions in the period 1803–05 alone at over 12,000 men, and Nelson suggested an improbably low figure of over 40,000 for the years 1793 to 1802. Captains could take some precautions against desertion by mooring midstream at a good distance from other ships in harbour, and by posting marine sentries and guard boats at night. If, notwithstanding these measures, a man succeeded in deserting his ship and evading recovery, an 'R' (for 'Run') was placed against his name in the ship's books, with all pay and prize money forfeited. Deserters apprehended and returned to their respective ships were flogged. Those found after a considerable passage of time were court-martialled and usually flogged around the fleet or hanged.

Leech explained that many seamen deserted,

> notwithstanding the great risk run by such a bold measure; for, if taken, they were sure to meet with a fearful retribution. Still,

many preferred the chance of freedom; some ran off when on shore with the boats, others dropped overboard in the night, and either swam on shore or were drowned. Many others were kept from running away by the strength of their attachment to their old messmates and by the hope of better days.

Desertion was particularly rife when a Royal Navy ship stood off an American port, for it was relatively simple for an Englishman to blend in among fellow-English speakers at a time when the distinctions between the accents of the two countries often remained blurred. With better conditions aboard American ships, particularly merchantmen, a British deserter could nearly always find employment there. Royal Navy captains, therefore, rarely permitted shore leave to their crews while anchored in American waters. Leech recorded:

> The principal draw-back on the enjoyment of our stay at Norfolk [Virginia], was the denial of liberty to go on shore. The strictest care was taken to prevent all communication with the shore, either personally or by letter. The reason of this prohibition was a fear lest we should desert. Many of our crew were Americans: some of these were pressed men; others were much dissatisfied with the severity, not to say cruelty, of our discipline; so that a multitude of the crew were ready to give 'leg bail,' as they termed it, could they have planted their feet on American soil. Hence our liberty was restrained.

Mutiny

The most serious crime a sailor could commit was mutiny, defined in Article 20 as treachery, sedition, refusal to obey legitimate orders and concealing the mutinous intentions of others. Conviction could be obtained only by court martial, and a sentence of death was invariably applied to leaders of a conspiracy. Hence, as Leech explained,

> To talk of mutiny on shore is an easy matter; but to excite it on shipboard is to rush on certain death. Let it be known that a man has dared to breathe the idea, and he is sure to swing at the yard-arm. Some of our men once saw six mutineers hanging at the yard-arm at once, in a ship whose crew exhibited the incipient beginnings of mutiny. Let mutiny be successful, the government will employ its whole force, if needful, in hunting down the mutineers; their blood, to the last drop, is the terrible retribution it demands for this offence.

Mutiny was rare, though dramatic, such as the case of the *Hermione* frigate, in which Captain Hugh Pigot, a cruel tyrant with little regard for the safety and well-being of his men, was murdered, together with most of the officers and midshipmen, in September 1797. The crew proceeded into a Spanish port in the West Indies, surrendering their vessel to the enemy. The *Hermione* was retaken two years later and those mutineers eventually caught were executed.

The most famous mutinies of the period were those occurring in the same year, at Spithead and the Nore. At the former station, the men

A: Clothing

8

6

7

2

3

1

4

5

A

B: Press gang

C: Weapons, ammunition and equipment

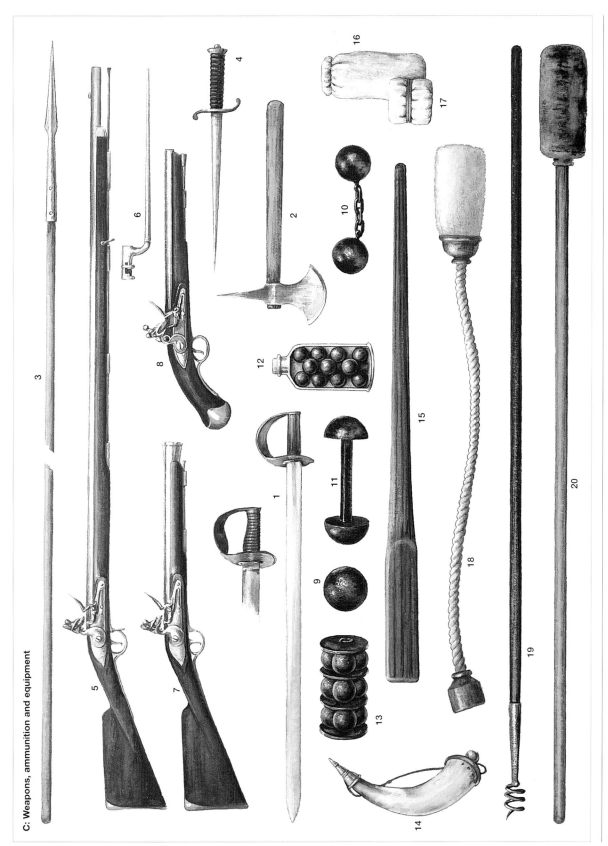

c

D: Swordsmanship

D

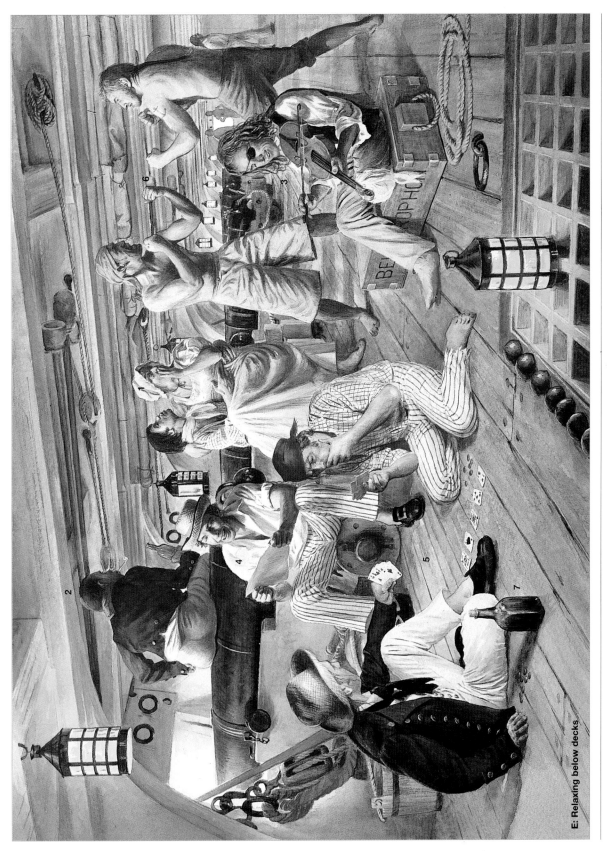

E: Relaxing below decks

E

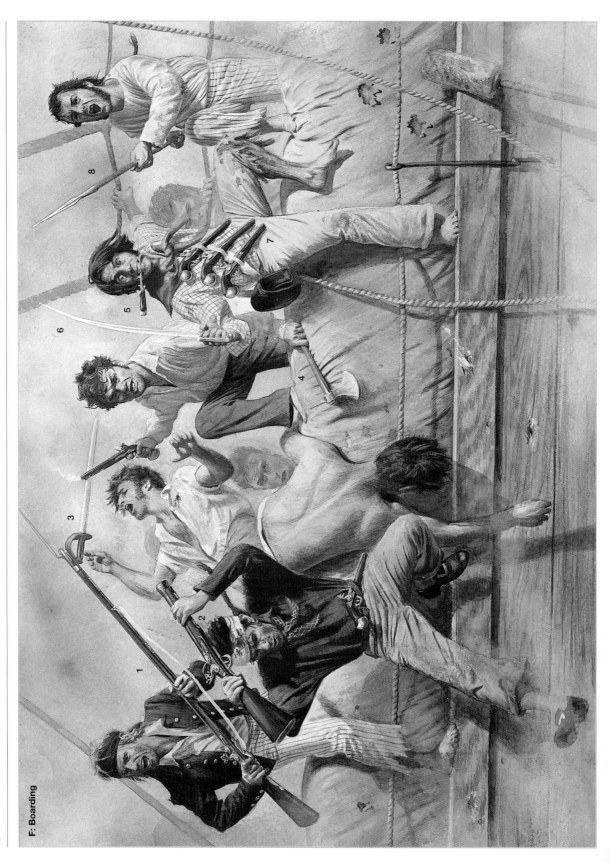

F: Boarding

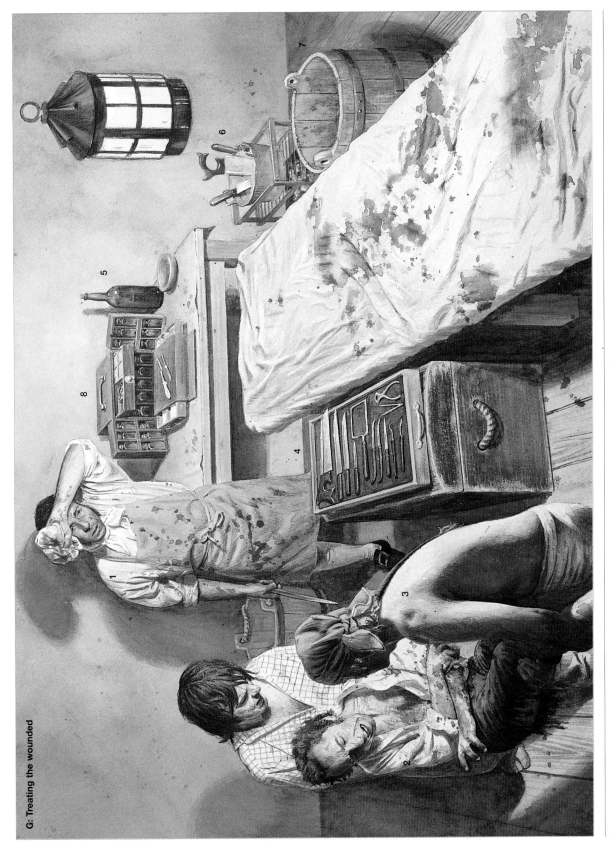

G: Treating the wounded

H: Preparing for battle

presented their demands, which included increased pay (unchanged since 1653), better food, pay for the injured and shore leave. The Admiralty conceded to their demands and, despite some violence, the mutiny passed without disruption. At the Nore, however, the crews blockaded London and demanded more extensive concessions, including a more equitable distribution of prize money. Squabbling among the mutineers eventually led Richard Parker, their leader, to surrender. He and 35 others were hanged. Others were sentenced to be flogged around the fleet or received prison terms.

SICKNESS, DISEASE AND DEATH

Ordinary seamen who required the surgeon's attention were seen in their hammocks or in the 'sick bay' or 'sick berth', which was nothing more than a small area separating the hammocks by a screen in the after part of the lower deck in a ship of the line, and on the gun deck, forward of the wardroom, in a frigate. This was far from ideal, so that after the turn of the century the Markham sick berth became commonplace. This was placed forward on the upper deck under the forecastle, and contained a dispensary and toilet, the whole supplied with light and circulating air. The sick received the ordinary food of the ship, if they could bear it, or 'portable soup', which consisted of a stock made by boiling beef, water and vegetables until reduced to a concentrate, then issued to each man at 1oz to 1qt of water per day. Those in the sick bay could redeem their missed portions of grog once discharged.

In battle the surgeon worked in the cockpit, situated on the orlop deck, using the midshipmen's table if available, or their sea chests lashed together. Wounded men were seen in the order in which they appeared for attention, and though many died in consequence of this illogical system, a skilful surgeon could perform an amputation with remarkable speed – sometimes in as little as two or three minutes. Speed was essential, not simply to save the man from bleeding to death, but to allow time to attend to all the other cases, whose numbers could at times be overwhelming. One surgeon, for instance, wrote of receiving 90 patients during a battle:

> The whole cockpit deck, cabins, wing berths and part of the cable tier, together with my platform and my preparations for dressing were covered with them ... Melancholy calls for assistance were addressed to me from every side by wounded and dying, and piteous moaning and bewailing from pain and despair.

One seaman described the cockpit in the midst of battle in similarly horrifying terms:

> The surgeon and his mate were smeared with blood from head to foot. They looked more like butchers than doctors ... The task was most painful to behold, the surgeon using his knife and saw on human flesh and bones as freely as the butcher at the shambles.

Men under the knife could expect to be cut with or probed by various instruments, including saws, knives, retractors, forceps, pincers and needles. Anaesthetics in the modern sense were unknown at the time, leaving only rum and laudanum as crude alternatives, plus a gag or a piece of leather-covered chain to grip between the teeth.

Contrary to popular belief, death in battle accounted for only a tiny fraction of fatalities suffered by men in the Royal Navy. Of the approximately 100,000 men who died during the French Revolutionary and Napoleonic Wars, only about 1.5 per cent died in action, 12 per cent as a result of shipwreck or other form of disaster, 20 per cent from accidents, and almost two-thirds from disease. However, great improvements over time in diet and sanitary conditions drastically reduced the number of deaths caused by disease.

Nevertheless sailors were subject to an array of injuries, diseases and other afflictions. Injuries took the form of fractures caused by a fall or concussion when a man banged his head against a low deck beam, or from falling objects. The regular and sustained lifting of heavy objects led to internal ruptures and hernias. Seasickness – unpleasant yet harmless – was the most common complaint. Leech recalled how, 'we who were landsmen had our share of that merciless, nondescript, hateful, stultifying disease, ycleped sea-sickness; as usual, we wished the foolish wish that we had never come to sea; as usual, we got over it, and laughed at ourselves for our sea-sick follies.' Infection also accounted for many illnesses and death, as exposed cuts, injuries and wounds were prone to become septic and possibly develop into gangrene or tetanus, which in turn could result in death.

Venereal diseases were commonplace, as was scurvy, an age-old affliction associated with life at sea, in which men experienced a deficiency in vitamins through the absence of fresh fruit and vegetables. Scurvy was almost eliminated after 1795 by the compulsory consumption of lemon or lime juice, issued each day with the rum ration (and hence the origin of the nickname 'limeys' given to British sailors).

Far worse, however, was what was then known as ship fever, better known today as typhus, which was spread by lice. Every man newly entered on to the ship's books was inspected for evidence of disease or ill-health generally, but typhus appeared regularly and could devastate a ship, particularly those designated to receive new recruits or pressed men, who as described earlier were forced to live below, under guard, in filthy conditions. Scrubbing the decks with vinegar, boiling a man's clothes and delousing him went some way towards eradicating the problem, but in this period no permanent solution was found to rid a ship's company of its verminous companions.

Other diseases were easily spread owing to cramped conditions: influenza and consumption could break out, while in tropical climates malaria, cholera and yellow fever struck with deadly frequency. Midshipman George Jackson described the symptoms of the last of these killers:

> Its real nature can be conceived only by those who have witnessed its horrors. The Spaniards call it 'vomits' from the black vomit that nearly always ensues, after which there is little or no hope of the patient's recovery. When attacked by this accursed retching, the sufferer frequently springs up in his bed and expels the dark thick

fluid from his mouth several feet beyond him in a moment of intense agony; and at times the patient is suddenly seized with such violent convulsions that the force of several powerful men is hardly sufficient to hold him down. This singular malady is so deceptive that the patient will sink at intervals into a calm and apparently refreshing sleep, as still as a child's slumber, and start suddenly thence without the slightest warning into one of those terrible fits.

There was also a variation of this called yellow jack, a combination of yellow fever and jaundice; malaria was a disease connected with swamps and tropical climates and particularly prevalent in the Caribbean. Men often dreaded news that they would be sent on a West Indian station.

On shore a sailor could receive treatment from physicians (that is, doctors with medical degrees), in addition to surgeons. A hospital with a capacity for 2,000 patients was located in Portsmouth, and one at Plymouth (opened in 1806) could care for over 1,000 patients. These establishments were maintained by the Navy Board, which deducted sixpence per month from every seaman's wages for the purpose. In addition to formal hospitals, smaller ports used hulks as hospital ships.

Funerals at sea were simple and quick: the man was sewn into his hammock with one or two round shot placed at his feet. The last stitch was sewn through his nose to ensure he was actually dead. The ship's company assembled by divisions and listened as the captain read the service before the body was committed to the deep. Leech recounted the standard procedure for the disposal of the dead:

> at sundown the ship's bell pealed a melancholy note, the ship was 'hove to,' all hands mustered on deck … and, amid the most profound silence, the body of the departed sailor was laid upon the grating and launched into the great deep, the resting-place of many a bold head. A plunge, a sudden opening in the water, followed by an equally sudden return of the disparted waves, and Black Tom was gone forever from his shipmates!

In action, bodies were thrown overboard as soon as possible, for they impeded movement about the decks. After the battle, the dead man's

Seamen enjoying a period of liberty ashore. Dissipation and excess characterized the conduct of sailors on leave. (Philip Haythornthwaite)

possessions were sold at auction on the upper deck, the proceeds being passed to his widow or next of kin.

LEAVE, LEISURE AND AMUSEMENTS

Leave
No right of leave existed for seamen, and on completing a commission they could be 'turned over' – that is, have their terms of service extended – or they might find themselves distributed among the crews of other ships. Leave was granted for trusted men or when the vessel docked in a foreign port, and sailors on liberty often dressed in their finest outfits and delighted in spending their money. Returning to a home port, in particular, generated enormous excitement aboard ship, as Leech recalled:

> Visions of many an old fire-side, of many a humble hearth-stone, poor, but precious, flitted across the visions of our crew that night. Hardships, severe discipline, were for the time forgotten in the dreams of hope … After running a few days before a fair wind, the delightful cry of 'Land ho!' was heard from the mast-head; a cry always pleasant to the inhabitant of a ship, but most especially so when the distant hills are those of his native land. Soon after the cry of the man aloft, the land became dimly visible from the deck, and our eyes glistened, as the bright, emerald fields of old England, in all the glory of their summer beauty, lay spread out before us.

Once on shore the men were almost certain to dissolve into excess, as many, especially those released from blockade duty, might not have enjoyed leave for more than a year.

Once in port, the men's conduct could sometimes get out of hand, and dissipation flourished. Samuel Stokes recalled one of the ships in which he sailed as 'noted for her wicked principles'. His particular vessel provided

> full scope to every sinful practice, for if ever there was anything on earth that deserved to be called a hell, this ship was one. But she was just what suited me, for I was only fit companion for the worst in the ship, and drunkenness and swearing was to me a delight … The sins of this ship was equal to the sins of Sodom, especially on the day we was paid, for we had on board thirteen women more than the number of our ship's company, and not fifty of them married women. Our ship's company, I think, was very near 800 men.

Leisure aboard ship
In the course of 24 hours the men had precious little time to themselves, this being confined to the four hours of the afternoon watch or the

Sailors carousing ashore. This print conveys something of the chaotic atmosphere into which many a seaside tavern dissolved when patronized by sailors on leave. (National Maritime Museum)

two hours of either of the dogwatches. This time was further reduced by the consumption of dinner and supper, so that only Sunday afternoon was theoretically reserved for leisure. Yet even this was subject to the whim of the captain and the traditions and routines kept by the ship. Men might spend their time in leisurely pursuits such as scrimshaw work, embroidering or skylarking. Scrimshaw involved the carving of ornaments from the bones of sea creatures, particularly whale or seal bone and shark teeth, but also walrus tusk or the vertebrae of any sea creature. Many men decorated their clothing through embroidery, which

usually involved sewing ribbons into the seams of shirts and trousers. Skylarking involved racing in, hanging from and playing in the rigging – naturally the favoured pursuit of the younger, fitter members of the crew. Tobacco was issued for a charge until 1798, and afterwards provided free at 2lb per month. Most men chewed rather than smoked it since the danger of fire below decks banned its use anywhere except in the galley or on the forecastle. Some men were fond of yarning, that is, the telling of tales of adventures, fables and ghost stories.

The men played various games, some permitted by Admiralty regulations, others not. Gambling, whether with cards or dice, was expressly forbidden by the Articles of War, though some captains turned a blind eye, often engaging in it themselves. Seamen also revelled in playing practical jokes on one another, and enjoyed 'grinning', contests in which a horse collar was worn around the neck of a man pulling hideous faces and for which prizes were given to the winner.

Sailors also liked to play instruments, such as the fiddle or fife, and danced jigs and hornpipes. Some men, using their spare time, made their own instruments with which to create music to accompany the many songs commemorating famous admirals and battles, some stretching back several centuries. A contemporary favourite went as follows:

Sailors relaxing, probably as their ship lies in port, as the presence of women suggests. Apart from Sunday afternoon there was precious little time for leisure. (Royal Naval Museum)

Main gun deck of a man-of-war at anchor off Gravesend. In this unusually orderly depiction of recreation aboard ship, seamen and their female companions drink and converse. The hammocks hanging from the beams offered the only form of (limited) privacy. (National Maritime Museum)

> Hearts of oak are our ships, jolly tars are our men,
> We always are ready, steady, boys, steady,
> To fight and to conquer again and again.

Leech recalled one sailor

> quite popular among them for his lively disposition and his talents as a comic singer, which last gift is always highly prized in a man of war … Seated on a gun surrounded by scores of the men, he sung a variety of favourite songs amid the plaudits and *encores* of his rough auditors.

Others told nautical yarns about past exploits and adventures, particularly to the younger members of the crew. Forbitters – songs sung around the forecastle – were often satirical and obscene, and enabled the men to criticize authority and lament their own circumstances without giving cause for rebuke.

The men particularly enjoyed the ritual associated with 'Crossing the Line', that is, passing over the Equator, which was supposed to signify that the world had turned upside down. Tradition demanded that any man who had not yet crossed the line had to undergo an initiation required by 'Neptune'. Suitably dressed in golden crown, flowing robe and long beard, and bearing a trident, a seaman in the guise of this ancient god of the sea would appear on the forecastle, accompanied by his wife, Amphitrite, and his chamberlain, Badger-Bag. Neptune's entourage included a surgeon, barber, nymphs and other bizarre creatures. The uninitiated were brought before the sea god, before whom was erected a bath made from a sheet of canvas or large barrel. A man could avoid further discomfort by paying a fine, classed as a tribute; otherwise, he was 'lathered' with tar or rancid grease, 'shaved' with a wooden spoon, and ducked in the artificial sea at Neptune's feet.

When in home waters or on permanent station, where a packet boat would have access to their ship, the men might also read letters from friends and family, or find another member of the crew to read them out, as most ordinary sailors were illiterate. Leech noted that

> The arrival of the mail-bag is a season of peculiar interest on board a man of war. It calls the finer feelings of human nature into exercise. It awakens conjugal, fraternal, and filial affection in almost every breast. The men crowd around, as the letters are distributed, and he was pronounced a happy fellow whose name was read off by the distributor …

Crossing the line. In this ritual, 'Neptune' enquires of each sailor whether he has ever passed over the Equator. As one captain described it, 'If he has, no more is said to him; but if he has not, he is then desired to do homage to the briny deep – which is being dipped in a bathing tub of seawater, or pay a fine of a bottle of rum to escape this sometimes very unmerciful ducking.' (Royal Naval Museum)

WOMEN

'There are', Leech declared,

> few worse places than a man of war, for the favourable development of the moral character of a boy. Profanity, in its most revolting aspect; licentiousness, in its most shameful and beastly garb; vice, in the worst of its Proteus-like shapes, abound there. While scarcely a moral restraint is thrown round the victim, the meshes of temptation are spread about his path in every direction.

In no respect was this more true than with regard to the sailors' conduct around women. No sooner than a ship arrived in port it was approached by boatloads of local women. The eagerness with which seamen, who had sometimes not seen a woman for months, welcomed these boats may well be imagined.

The appearance of these boats is easily explained: since leave for ordinary seamen (as opposed to officers) was only granted at the discretion of the captain – and this he often refused for fear of desertion – women were permitted to come aboard a ship in port so long as they did not bring alcohol, disrupt the proper functions of the vessel, and could provide *bona fide* proof of marriage. Of course, rarely were these criteria met, and captains generally accepted openly forged certificates.

The consequences were predictable: prostitutes in great numbers appeared in boats beside the ships at anchor, waiting to be chosen by sailors flush with cash. Sometimes literally hundreds of women occupied the decks, sharing hammocks with the men without regard to privacy or decency, and remaining on board for several days at a time, in the course of which period many men would contract or pass on gonorrhoea or syphilis.

Robinson described this extraordinary phenomenon:

> After having moored our ship, swarms of boats came round us; some were what are generally termed bomb-boats, but are really nothing but floating chandler's shops; and a great many of them were freighted with cargos of ladies, a sight that was truly gratifying, and a great treat: for our crew, consisting of six hundred and upwards, nearly all young men, had seen but one woman on board for eighteen months …
>
> So soon as these boats were allowed to come alongside, the seamen flocked down pretty quick, one after the other, and brought their choice up, so that in the course of the afternoon, we had about four hundred and fifty on board.
>
> Of all the human race, these poor young creatures are the most pitiable; the ill-usage and the degradation they are driven to submit to, are indescribable; but from habit they become callous, indifferent as to delicacy of speech and behaviour, and so totally lost to all sense of shame, that they seem to retain no quality which properly belongs to woman, but the shape and name.

George Watson was surprised to find that the nurses at Plymouth hospital claimed to have many husbands,

> … or men they called by that name, all living on board different ships … As there was seldom more than one of these in port at a time, they equally enjoyed the caresses of the pliable spouses in happy ignorance of their dishonour … These ladies are exceedingly bold … I had a great deal to do to repulse the temptations I met with from these sirens, the more so as I was naturally fond of the society of women.

Genuine wives, on the other hand, sometimes went to sea in small numbers with their husbands, and received pay for mending and washing clothes and other menial tasks. In action they supplied the gun crews with cartridges from the magazine or assisted the surgeon. Indeed, contemporary prints show women attending the wounded above and below decks, and at least two babies were born in battle, labour possibly induced by the excitement of events. Remarkably, Daniel Tremendous McKenzie, born aboard the 74-gun *Tremendous* during the battle of the Glorious First of June, received, at the age of 53, the Naval General Service Medal, with the rating of 'baby', for his presence in that engagement – surely a unique instance of a medal being awarded to a seaman for services performed on the day of his birth.

An unknown number of women disguised themselves as men in order to serve aboard ship. Before being discovered, Elizabeth Bowden spent six weeks aboard the 16-gun *Hazard* in 1807 as a boy third class. Another woman, entered into the books of the 100-gun *Queen Charlotte*, served at least 11 years as an able seaman and captain of the foretop before her true gender was revealed after the wars had ended in 1815.

EXPERIENCE OF BATTLE AND AFTERMATH

The course of a typical naval action, whether that action consisted of a duel between single vessels or a great contest between powerful fleets, followed a number of fairly consistent phases. First, an enemy ship, squadron or fleet would be sighted somewhere on the horizon through a lookout's telescope. It was his task to identify the nearest vessel by the shape of its hull and the types of sails she carried. Only later could he make out the ensign. If she flew the *tricolore* or the flag of a French ally, the captain normally ordered a pursuit, providing he was satisfied that the odds were in his favour. William Dillon, a 14-year-old gunner aboard the *Defence* in 1794, explained in his memoirs what happened on the first sighting of the enemy:

> Lord Howe made the signal to prepare for battle, and for the flying squadron to chace and engage the enemy. So soon as those signals were displayed to our ships, a state of excitement was manifested totally beyond my powers of description. No one thought of anything else than to exert himself to his utmost ability in overcoming the enemy. It was also very satisfactory to observe the change of disposition in the ship's company of the *Defence*. All animation and alacrity pervaded these men: no more sulky looks. The enemy was near, and all hands were determined to support their captain. The ships when near each other were cheered by their crews in succession. Death or Victory was evidently the prevailing feeling.

Once an enemy was identified, the captain called the 'beat to quarters', which meant that with the beating of a drum the crew sprang into action to prepare for battle. This meant more than merely ceasing whatever it was a man happened to be doing at the time. Hammocks were lashed and stowed away or lashed to the lower shrouds in order to protect the men from falling debris, splinters or even muskets balls during the fighting. Above the main deck the men fixed large nets to catch anything that might tumble from the rigging on to the busy deck: men, spars, yards – in short, anything aloft. More nets were placed on the ship's side to render more difficult any enemy attempt at boarding. As Dillon recalled, 'Whilst we were in chace, a splinter netting was fitted over the quarter deck to receive the blocks that might be shot away aloft, and a cask of water was hoisted into the main top, to be prepared for fire.'

This last procedure was meant to reduce the possibility of fire taking hold in the tops or rigging. Yet this threat posed more than a danger to the rigging alone; fanned by the wind, flames could easily spread to the ship herself with catastrophic results. Buckets of water were therefore pulled up and poured over the sails as a rudimentary flame retardant.

More buckets were left next to the guns and by the hatchways, and wet sand was cast over the decks to prevent men from slipping as the ship rolled and received fire. Any sails not needed were furled and lashed securely, particularly the mainsail. The yards, from which the sails were suspended, were then chained to the masts to secure them from crashing to the decks. All such measures were meant to minimize damage; the fact nevertheless remained that, if the weight and accuracy of enemy fire were great enough, little could be done to stop masts, spars and rigging from tumbling down like the branches of a tree in a storm.

Meanwhile, on the main deck and below, anything not necessary for fighting or that might interfere with operations had to be stowed below the waterline or cast overboard. The captain's furniture, for instance, was removed, together with the partitions of the officers' quarters. Any cows on board were slaughtered by the ship's butcher and their carcasses thrown over the side. Goats and chickens, along with their pens or coops, followed suit. The hens were preserved in the ships' boats and the pigs sent below to a section known as the 'manger' near the front of the vessel. Everything else was sent to the hold or heaved overboard – whatever its value. Nothing that could conceivably impede the men in battle was permitted to remain unsecured.

On the poop deck and forecastle the marines assembled with their muskets while others stood guard over the hatchways leading to the lower deck: no one could be allowed to desert his appointed station and seek the limited protection of the lower decks. On the orlop deck or in the cockpit (the after part of the orlop deck and normally the quarters of the midshipmen) the surgeon and his assistants laid out the medical instruments and generally converted the place into a makeshift hospital ward and operating theatre. A dining table was cleaned and covered, while above it were hung lanterns to facilitate the gruesome work of amputation and the extraction of splinters and musket balls. Sometimes a prayer was offered for divine protection and victory, and in the bustle the men sometimes made arrangements to transfer personal effects to their friends in the event of death. Sometimes a seaman agreed to throw his mate over the side if his wounds were grievous enough, thus avoiding inevitable suffering under the surgeon's knife.

Robinson records that in preparing for battle a ship's company would perform a set routine,

> such as breaking away the captain and officer's cabins, and sending all the lumber below – the doctors, parson, purser and loblolly men, were also busy, getting the medical chests and bandages out; and sails prepared for the wounded to be placed on, that they might be dressed in rotation, as

Boarding action. (National Maritime Museum)

they were taken down to the after cock-pit. In such a bustling, and it may be said, trying as well as serious time, it is curious to notice the different dispositions of the British sailor. Some would be offering a guinea for a glass of grog, whilst others were making a sort of mutual will, such as, if one of Johnny Crapeau's shots (a term given to the French), knocks my head off, you will take all my effects; and if you are killed, and I am not, why, I will have yours, and this is generally agreed to.

Second Lieutenant Ellis of the marines, aboard the *Ajax* at Trafalgar, left a description of events below decks before the action:

I was sent below with orders and was much struck with the preparations made by the bluejackets [seamen], the majority of whom were stripped to the waist; a handkerchief was tightly bound round their heads and over their ears, to deaden the noise of the cannon, many men being deaf for days after an action. The men were variously occupied – some were sharpening their cutlasses, others polishing the guns, as though an inspection were about to take place instead of a mortal combat, whilst three or four, as if in mere bravado, were dancing a hornpipe. Occasionally they would look out of the ports and speculate as to the various ships of the enemy, many of which had been on former occasions engaged by our vessels.

Elsewhere, the carpenter and his assistants gathered materials used for plugging shot holes made to the hull near or below the waterline. These men would also move about the ship to repair any damage that prevented or slowed the fighting efficiency of the ship. The master gunner, meanwhile, opened the magazine, which contained the ship's store of ammunition and powder. The men who worked there wore special felt slippers and carefully avoided carrying anything metal: the slightest spark could ignite the powder and destroy the ship. Blankets

Gun crew in action. The standard of gunnery in the Royal Navy easily surpassed that of other European navies, though it was perhaps equalled by the Americans, who gave a good account of themselves in the conflict of 1812–15. (Royal Naval Museum)

hung in the doorway to the magazine were soaked with water and a marine guard was posted at the entrance. Young boys known as 'powder monkeys' were issued with powder cartridges to be conveyed to each of the guns. Any fire burning in the galley was extinguished and the ship's officers ensured that in all respects the ship was ready for action.

Most of the crew, both above and below deck, manned the guns, with their officers standing by ready to issue orders. All of their equipment and ammunition was carefully checked. At Trafalgar, the men of the *Bellerophon* chalked the words 'Victory or Death' in large letters on their guns. The gunners opened the ports, loaded their weapons and ran them out on both sides of the ship.

Once the guns were ready to fire and the men appropriately armed, the captain often toured the decks, inspecting preparations and offering a few words to raise the men's spirits before action commenced. Dillon remembers how his own captain

> went round the ship and spoke to all the men at their guns in terms of encouragement, to fight for their country. The replies he received were gratifying in the highest degree. The noblest feelings of patriotism were proclaimed, with expressions of the warmest enthusiasm: in short, a determination to conquer prevailed throughout the ship – and, I may as well say, throughout the British fleet.

This final, important task completed, the captain placed himself on the quarterdeck behind the mainmast with his signal officers and other staff subordinates assembled around him. All this and more was accomplished in a matter of minutes. The ship was now ready to fight and the men waited anxiously until the enemy vessel came within range. Sometimes this could take hours if the distance was great, the wind was unfavourable or the enemy managed to evade action.

In the meantime, the men were sometimes fed, as Lieutenant Cumby of the *Bellerophon* observed shortly before the fighting at Trafalgar. 'Finding we should not be in action for an hour or more, we piped to dinner, thinking that Englishmen would fight all the better for having a comfortable meal'. Aboard the *Victory*, Able Seaman John Brown remembered that the crew ate 'a bit of salt pork and half a pint of wine' before action began. Aboard the *Tonnant*, Able Seaman John Cash recalled that:

> Our good captain called all hands and said, 'My lads, this will be a glorious day for us and the groundwork of a speedy return to our homes.' He then ordered bread and cheese and butter for every man at the guns. I was one of them, and, believe me, we ate and drank, and were as cheerful as ever we had been over a pot of beer.

Still others would take a drink or say a prayer.

Dillon described the opening of one such action thus:

> Shortly after 9 o'clock we were getting very near to our opponents. Up went their lower deck ports, out came the guns,

and the fire on us commenced from several of the enemy's van ships … We retained our fire till in the act of passing under the Frenchman's stern, then, throwing all our topsails aback, luffed up and poured in a most destructive broadside. We heard most distinctly our shot striking the hull of the enemy. The carved work over his stern was shattered to pieces. Then, ranging up alongside him within half a pistol shot distance, our fire was kept up with the most determined spirit.

Working the guns was hard, physical work, for they weighed over 1,000lb each and had to be manhandled back into position after every discharge. Most of the work involved sponging, loading, aiming and firing, the last of which brought with it a tremendous roar and a cloud of smoke that often shrouded the gun deck and adversely affected not only hearing but also breathing and sight. The force of the explosion created a violent recoil, driving the gun back until it was abruptly stopped by ropes and side tackles. Without these a 'loose cannon' – from which the metaphor is derived – would career back into the men or roll across the deck, crushing anything and anyone in its path. As the gun crews did their work, officers stood by to ensure men kept their places and performed their functions with maximum efficiency. Yet even veteran crews could find this a ghastly and unnerving experience, marked by deafening noise, swirling, choking smoke and shouting men – all heightened by the very real prospect of horrendous injury or death.

Marine Second Lieutenant Rotely in the *Victory* at Trafalgar described the action thus:

We were engaging on both sides; every gun was going off. A man should witness a battle in a three-decker from the middle deck, for it beggars all description: it bewilders the senses of sight and hearing. There was the fire from above, the fire from below, besides the fire from the deck I was upon, the guns recoiling with violence, reports louder than thunder, the decks heaving and the sides straining. I fancied myself in the infernal regions, where every man appeared a devil. Lips might move, but orders and hearing were out of the question; everything was done by signs.

Indeed, soon enough some enemy shot would inevitably reach their targets. Projectiles aimed at a ship's rigging, such as chain shot, shredded sails and left lines tangled or severed, while solid iron shot damaged or carried away spars and masts. Dillon recalled how 'a volley of shot assailed the poop, cut away the main brace, and made sad havoc there'. Round shot directed at the hull, particularly at short distances, could penetrate it, carrying with it a cloud of sharp splinters in all directions, dislodging guns and striking down men like bowling pins. A man who was lucky enough to survive being struck by a shot usually only did so at the cost of an appendage either shattered or carried away. Occasionally a shot would enter an open port unimpeded by the thick sides of the ship and was thus all the more lethal.

Even if a seaman remained unscathed, the sudden and powerful rush of air produced by a passing ball could knock him over, a phenomenon known as 'wind of ball'. Dillon noted how

> two of the men were blown down from the wind of a shot from the ship we were engaging, and I was carried away with them by the shock. I thought myself killed, as I became senseless, being jammed between these men. So soon as the smoke cleared away, our companions noticed my situation. They came, lugged me out, and began rubbing my limbs. This brought me to my senses.

Robinson recorded how at Trafalgar the enemy shot 'were whistling over us, some a-head, some a-stern, and a great many fell short …

Boarding action. A boarding party, even if outnumbered, stood a reasonable chance of success provided the opposing vessel had been thoroughly battered by cannon fire as a preparatory measure. The issue was usually decided in a matter of minutes within the confines of the upper decks. (National Maritime Museum)

Amongst them was a very distressing and mischievous one, which knocked a man's head completely from his shoulders.'

Thus, once battle was joined, in a short space of time the reality of combat manifested itself in a horrifying combination of men shouting on their feet, the wounded screaming on their backs and the dead sprawled lifeless – and often mangled – in bloody heaps. Dillon recorded the shocking spectacle of death. 'I had never seen a man killed before,' he recalled of an action in 1794.

It was a most trying scene. A splinter struck him in the crown of the head, and when he fell the blood and brains came out, flowing over the deck. The captain went over, and, taking the poor fellow by the hand, pronounced him dead. The others, who were wounded, were taken below to the surgeon.

A few days later, at a more ferocious encounter with the French, Dillon witnessed the death of another seaman:

One of these was John Polly, of very short stature, who remarked that as he was so small the shot would all pass over him. The words had not been long out of his mouth when a shot cut his head right in two, leaving the tip of each ear remaining on the lower part of the cheek. His sudden death created a sensation among his comrades, but the excitement of the moment soon changed those impressions to others of exertion. There was no withdrawing from our situation, and the only alternative was to face the danger with becoming firmness. The head of this unfortunate seaman was cut so horizontally that anyone looking at it would have supposed it had been done by the blow of an axe. His body was committed to the deep.

Robinson recalled that at Trafalgar one of his shipmates narrowly escaped being mistaken for dead and thrown overboard. The ship's cobbler

happened to be stationed at the gun where this messenger of death and destruction [a double-headed shot] entered [the gun port], and the poor fellow was so completely stunned by the head of another man being knocked against his, that no one doubted but that he was dead. As it is customary to throw overboard those, who, in an engagement are killed outright, the poor cobbler, amongst the rest, was taken to the port-hole to be committed to the deep, without any other ceremony than shoving him through the port: but, just as they were about to let him slip from their hands into the water, the blood began to circulate, and he commenced kicking. Upon this sign of returning life, his shipmates soon hauled the poor snob in again, and though wonderful to relate, he recovered so speedily, that he actually fought the battle out.

If a man were injured he might be fortunate enough to find himself carried below to the surgeon on the orlop deck. Captain Bayntun of the

Leviathan, fighting at Trafalgar, observed how one seaman showed extraordinary stoicism under the circumstances:

> A shot took off the arm of Thomas Main, when at his gun on the forecastle; his messmates kindly offered to assist him in going to the Surgeon; but he bluntly said, 'I thank you, stay where you are; you will do more good there;' he then went down by himself to the cockpit. The Surgeon would willingly have attended him, in preference to others, whose wounds were less alarming; but Main would not admit it, saying, 'Avast, not until it comes to my turn, if you please.' The Surgeon soon amputated the shattered part of the arm; during which, with great composure, smiling, and with a steady clear voice, he sang the whole of 'Rule Britannia.'

Throughout the fighting, the pumps were manned to prevent the ship from sinking, and there was always the threat of fire or – far more catastrophic – explosion, if an enemy shot happened to penetrate the magazine. Such instances were rare, but the result was usually the loss of all hands. Generally speaking, rival ships simply pounded each other until one surrendered, known as striking the colours. A particularly determined crew might fight on until their ship was nothing more than a scarcely floating hulk, stripped of its masts and fearfully reduced in fighting men. Naval battles need not, however, prove fights to the finish. In a typical fleet action ships were normally lost or taken, but fighting usually ceased when one side, for any of a host of reasons, chose to disengage and withdraw from the battle, abandoning those of its ships that were crippled or captured. Until such time the contest continued as each ship sought to bring its broadside to bear on the enemy vessel closest to hand.

Dillon offers further details of the kind of destruction wrought by the massed firepower of a ship of the line. In his account of the Glorious First of June, the first major naval action of the French Revolutionary Wars, he noted how, after a heated struggle, 'the main mast came down on the starboard side of the poop with a terrible crash'. Men in the tops 'reported the upper end of the quarter deck to be dreadfully shattered'. Below, meanwhile, the

> lower deck was at times so completely filled with smoke that we could scarcely distinguish each other, and the guns were so heated that, when fired, they nearly kicked the upper deck beams. The metal became so hot that, fearing some accident, we reduced the quantity of powder, allowing also more time to elapse between the loading and firing of them.

If the ships were close enough, grape shot – a bundle of musket balls bound together by a canvas bag – was used to clear the enemy deck like a giant shotgun. On deck the wounded were carried below down gangways watched by vigilant marines, ready to shoot any man who sought unauthorized access to the lower reaches of the ship. Indeed, there was scarcely anywhere for a man to run if he wanted to, for only the powder monkeys, the wounded and their bearers were permitted to go below. Once the injured were left on the orlop deck their able-bodied

bearers returned to their guns. There, meanwhile, officers stood by, ready to strike down or shoot any man who deserted his post. This was seldom the case aboard British vessels, yet in the heat and confusion of action even the most obedient and willing men could sometimes lose their concentration or nerve, and warrant officers frequently resorted to shouts and shoves to keep such men focused on the critical task in hand.

When a battle ended, men immediately took stock of the damage, human and material. Dillon described the aftermath of battle aboard the *Defence* thus:

> It was past 12 o'clock, and I concluded the fighting part of our duty to be at an end. My clothes were still damp: my shoes, to which I had small buckles, were covered with blood; my face and hands smutched with powder and blood.

Robinson, describing the aftermath of Trafalgar, recalled how

> We were now called to clear the decks, and here might be witnessed an awful and interesting scene, for as each officer and seaman would meet … they were inquiring for their mess-mates. Orders were now given to fetch the dead bodies from the after cock-pit, and throw them over-board; these were the bodies of men who were taken down to the doctor during the battle, badly wounded, and who by the time the engagement was ended were dead.

Yet there was much more to do than merely seek out survivors. Shattered rigging was thrown overboard; holes were plugged; masts and spars were repaired, where possible; and sails had to be mended. In short, the ship had to be rendered as seaworthy as possible. More extensive repairs could be made on reaching a friendly port. At the same time, repairs of a very different nature carried on below, where the wounded continued to be tended on the entirely illogical basis of 'first come, first served'. There, unlike everywhere else, rank quite properly held no special privilege, yet without a system of triage, a more serious case often waited its turn behind more minor injuries. It is therefore not surprising that many a severely wounded seaman needlessly died under this regime.

Robinson relates the story of one such sailor, both of whose calves were shot away by a single shot:

> It became necessary to amputate one of the legs immediately, and during the operation he did not utter a syllable; and shortly after, on the doctor's examining the other leg, that was also doomed to undergo a similar fate; upon being told this, the poor fellow pleaded very hard that it might be left him, and very coolly observed that he should like one leg left to wear his shoes out, but the doctor was obliged to take off the other leg, the symptoms of mortification being very apparent: like a brave fellow, he bore his sufferings with great fortitude … This man was progressively doing well, and his wounds were healing fast; but, from lying in one position for such a length of time, his back mortified, and he breathed his last, much regretted by all his shipmates.

The fate of the dead was dictated by necessity: men who had been killed in action on the lower decks or who died of their wounds on the orlop were often unceremoniously dropped into the water through the ports. Those found slain on deck were similarly heaved overboard. Some, at least, were not buried at sea until their friends had had a brief opportunity to say a few words of gratitude and regret.

There might also be survivors – including enemy sailors – clinging to wreckage in the water, who needed to be rescued.

Finally, with the decks cleared of debris, the dead disposed of and the blood washed away, the roll was taken, losses assessed and food and water distributed. 'I helped to save a black pig which swam over,' Robinson wrote of his experiences at Trafalgar, 'and what a glorious supper of pork chops appeared instead of our usual refection of cheese, biscuit and salt junk.' So began the process by which the men could recover from the strains of combat, settle back to the routine of life at sea and await the next opportunity for battle.

MUSEUMS AND PLACES OF INTEREST

There are several sites connected with the subject of this book that readers are recommended to visit. The National Maritime Museum in Greenwich, south-west London, contains numerous displays, objects and paintings focusing on the Royal Navy of Nelson's day and the officers and men who made Britain the foremost maritime power of the era. The Royal Naval Museum in Portsmouth, Hampshire, not only maintains an excellent collection of artefacts, but stands immediately opposite the beautifully preserved HMS *Victory*, which lies in dry dock and is open to the public. A great deal about sailors' lives during the French Revolutionary and Napoleonic Wars can be learned by the independent exploration of Nelson's flagship, or through a guided tour of the same. Those wishing to find out more about the construction of Royal Navy ships are urged to visit Chatham Historic Dockyard, in Kent, and Buckler's Hard, in Hampshire.

BIBLIOGRAPHY

Baynham, Henry, *From the Lower Deck*, Hutchinson, London (1969)

Blake, Nicholas and Richard Lawrence, *The Illustrated Companion to Nelson's Navy*, Chatham Publishing, London (1999)

Dillon, William Henry, *A Narrative of my Professional Adventures (1790–1839)*, edited by M. A. Lewis, Navy Records Society, London, Vols. 93 and 97 (1953, 1956)

Ellis, Lady (ed.), *Memoirs and Services of the Late Lieutenant-General Sir S. B. Ellis KCB, Royal Marines, from his own Memoranda*, Saunders, Otley, London (1866)

Fabb, John and Jack Cassin-Scott, *The Uniforms of Trafalgar*, B. T. Batsford, London (1977)

Goodwin, Peter, *Men O'War: The Illustrated Story of Life in Nelson's Navy*, National Maritime Museum, London (2004)

Goodwin, Peter, *Nelson's Victory: 101 Questions & Answers about HMS Victory, Nelson's Flagship at Trafalgar 1805*, Conway Maritime Press, London (2004)

Hart, Roger, *England Expects*, Wayland Publishers, London (1972)

A typical seaman of the Royal Navy. (Philip Haythornthwaite)

Haythornthwaite, Philip, *Nelson's Navy*, Osprey Publishing, Oxford (1999)

Keevil, J. J., Christopher Lloyd and Jack Coulter, *Medicine and the Navy 1200–1900*, 3 vols., E & S Livingstone, Edinburgh (1957)

King, Dean, *A Sea of Words: A Lexicon and Companion for Patrick O'Brian's Seafaring Tales*, Henry Holt, London (2001)

King, Dean and Hattendorf, John B. (eds), *Every Man Will Do His Duty: An Anthology of First-Hand Accounts from the Age of Nelson, 1793–1815*, Conway Maritime Press, London (1997)

Lavery, Brian, *Jack Aubrey Commands: An Historical Companion to the Naval World of Patrick O'Brian*, Conway Maritime Press, London (2003)

Lavery, Brian, *Nelson's Navy: The Ships, Men and Organisation, 1793–1815*, Conway Maritime Press, London (1992)

Lavery, Brian, *Shipboard Life and Organisation, 1731–1815*, Ashgate, London (1999)

Leech, Samuel, *A Voice from the Main Deck: Being a Record of the Thirty Years Adventures of Samuel Leech*, Chatham Publishing, London (1999; reprint of 1857 edition)

Lewis, Jon E. (ed.), *The Mammoth Book of Life Before the Mast*, Robinson, London (2001)

Lewis, Michael A., *A Social History of the Navy, 1793–1815*, George Allen & Unwin, London (1960)

Lovell, William Stanhope, *Personal Narrative of Events, 1799–1815*, William Allen, London (1879)

Macdonald, Janet, *Feeding Nelson's Navy: The True Story of Food at Sea in the Georgian Era*, Chatham Publishing, London (2004)

Masefield, John, *Sea Life in Nelson's Time*, Conway Maritime Press, London (1971)

Maynard, C. (ed.), *A Nelson Companion: A Guide to the Royal Navy of Jack Aubrey*, Michael O'Mara Books, London (2004)

Nicol, John, *Memoirs of John Nicol*, edited by Alexander Laing, Cassell, London (1937)

Pope, Dudley, *Life in Nelson's Navy*, Chatham Publishing, London (1997)

Pope, Stephen, *Hornblower's Navy: Life at Sea in the Age of Nelson*, Welcome Rain, London (1998)

Robinson, William, *Jack Nastyface: Memoirs of an English Seaman*, Chatham Publishing, Rochester, Kent (2002; reprint of 1836 edition)

Rodger, N. A. M., *The Wooden World: An Anatomy of the Georgian Navy*, Fontana Press, London (1988)

COLOUR PLATE COMMENTARY

A: CLOTHING

In contrast to the officers and marines, no uniform existed for ordinary sailors of this period. When a man first entered a ship he initially continued to wear his own clothes, gradually replaced by 'slops' – either cloth or actual clothes from the ship's purser, and which the men could buy or be ordered to buy, on credit, at the equivalent of two months' pay. Any degree of uniformity among a ship's company was usually the result of bulk purchasing of clothing on the part of the purser or a product of the captain's own personal desire for some sort of standard outfit, although this was rare, and the Admiralty laid down no requirements for such. At the very least, some captains issued a standard form of headgear to their crew, which sometimes bore the name of the ship either painted on the front (the origin of the modern practice) or embroidered on a ribbon tied around the hat. Sailors were versatile, by necessity, and could use a needle and thread, not only to repair what clothes they had, but to fashion new ones from material they purchased.

Notwithstanding the lack of uniformity among the sailors, a captain expected his crew to look smart, and if there was anything constituting a standard outfit (**1**) it was a practical, short, usually blue, jacket without tails (being less restrictive than a long coat), with a double row of brass buttons running down the front, and buttoning cuffs, which enabled the sleeves to be rolled up when working. This was sometimes accompanied by a waistcoat, worn over a plain or checked white shirt (**2**), and white or off-white loose-fitting trousers (**3**), sometimes striped, and cut very wide so that they could be rolled up to the ankles or knees, thus allowing free movement. The sailor preferred a small-brimmed hat to a cocked one, often round, either of straw or felt and glazed to protect the head from cold weather. Black leather shoes (**4**), with or without square silver or gold buckles, were commonplace, but were usually dispensed with by seamen except when ashore or going aloft. Clothes were expected to be kept clean with the aid of sea water, but without soap, washed in a wooden basin (**5**). For ordinary duties and particularly in battle many men favoured a headscarf (**6**), which varied in colour and often bore designs in the form of stripes, dots or checks. When he went ashore a sailor liked to look smart; his best jacket (**7**) might therefore sport additional embellishments such as piping in yellow or gold. A clay pipe (**8**) was a common accessory of the British tar.

B: PRESS GANG

Whether shore-based or improvised from a ship's crew, a press gang on patrol in the streets of a port town kept a keen eye out for prime seamen on leave from merchant vessels or from naval vessels laid up and out of service. Here, a sailor (**1**), recently released, and still in his 'shore-going rig', might have evaded a press gang had he changed into the 'long clothes' of a landsman. Even this expedient might not suffice, for if a man showed no outward appearance of being a seaman or denied any connection with shipping, the gang might inspect his hands for evidence of tar – an

Sailors landed during the expedition to Buenos Aires in 1807 celebrate their success amid their booty. Seamen were sometimes ordered ashore to assist in amphibious operations or to supply the army by river or sea. (Royal Naval Museum)

unmistakable mark of a sailor. When he was, however, easily distinguishable by his attire and not registered on a warship's books he was very much at risk of being seized in this officially sanctioned form of kidnapping.

The law required that a press gang be led by an officer (**2**) holding the king's commission, and also carrying a warrant to impress men, signed by the Lords of the Admiralty. This understandably carries no authority with the victim's wife and young children (**3**), who plead for the return of their husband and father. Such entreaties were invariably fruitless, for press gangs gave no consideration to a man's domestic circumstances and stood to profit for each man they collared.

On accosting a man with a nautical air about him, violence was resorted to if necessary, either with cudgels or fists (**4**). One seaman recorded how in London a gang member

gave a whistle and in a moment I was in the hands of six or eight ruffians whom I immediately dreaded and soon found to be a press gang. They dragged me hurriedly along through several streets amid bitter execrations bestowed on them, expressions of sympathy directed towards me and landed me in one of their houses of rendezvous.

C: WEAPONS, AMMUNITION AND EQUIPMENT

Seamen used a variety of weapons for close-quarter fighting while boarding or repelling boarders. Small arms were

Seized up to the rigging. Usually reserved for recalcitrant midshipmen, but also inflicted on the ratings, this punishment involved spread-eagled suspension to the shrouds for hours at a time, exposing the prisoner to wind and rain. (Royal Naval Museum)

divided between firearms and edged weapons. The cutlass (**1**), with a straight blade, was produced with a variety of grips and guards and proved most effective when used to thrust rather than to slash. The tomahawk, or boarding axe (**2**), resembled the weapon used by North American Indians. Its curved, wedge-shaped blade made it ideal in hand-to-hand combat for, like the pike, it could be easily extracted from its victim. Moreover, when boarders experienced difficulty ascending the side of an enemy vessel, those bearing axes could drive the sharp spike on the back of the blade into the side of the ship so as to fashion makeshift ladders. It was also useful in cutting away rigging. The pike (**3**), which was employed exclusively for stabbing or jabbing, came in two lengths, a full-length version measuring over 7ft, and a half-pike for more confined spaces, measuring 4ft. Pikes were usually mounted at the base of the masts where they were close at hand when needed. The dirk (**4**) was usually the preserve of midshipmen, but ordinary sailors sometimes carried them. This had a blade longer than a dagger yet shorter than a sword.

Firearms consisted of the smooth-bore sea-service flintlock musket (**5**), a slightly shorter model than its army counterpart, but also capable of carrying a bayonet (**6**), the wide-mouthed blunderbuss (**7**) and the pistol (**8**). From the deck of a rolling ship or from his position in the rigging a musket-armed seaman was extremely lucky to hit his target at 100yds. At 50yds he had a more realistic chance of success.

The principal types of projectile fired by cannons (officially 'long' or 'great' guns), were round shot (**9**), the standard form of ammunition, cast in solid iron, used to batter the enemy's hull or to bombard shore batteries. Chain shot (**10**) consisted of two round shot (or one shot divided in half) linked by a short chain. This projectile damaged masts, yards, rigging and sails. Another form of ammunition used to hinder the

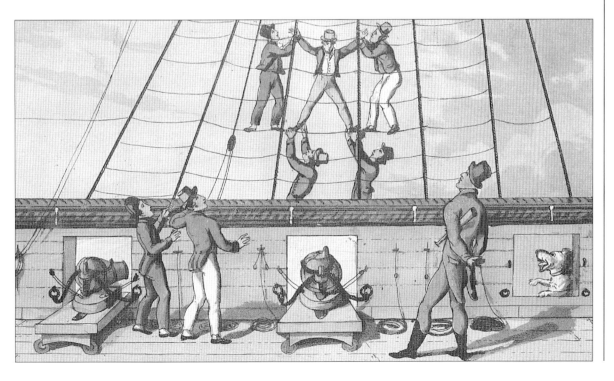

Capture of *La Chiffonne*, 19 August 1801. (Angus Konstam)

progress of an enemy vessel, bar shot (**11**), was two halves of a shot connected by a short bar. Canister shot (**12**) consisted of a cylindrical tin or iron container, holding a collection of small iron balls centred around a wooden stem in the centre. This proved effective against rigging and men alike. Grape shot (**13**) consisted of iron balls resting around an iron spindle, which was sewn into a canvas bag. When fired, shot spread out like shotgun pellets, being particularly effective against enemy boarders and gun crews.

The powder horn (**14**) contained a fine-quality black powder used for priming a gun. This priming powder was poured down the vent – the touch hole at the breech end of the gun – and when lit it ignited the main charge, causing the explosion that fired the gun. The handspike (**15**) was a wooden stave, whose square end was used to lever the gun carriage into a proper position in which to fire, especially after the recoil caused by the previous discharge. The cartridge (**16**), or 'charge', was a canvas bag containing a certain measure of black powder, determined by the size of the projectile to be fired. This was inserted in the muzzle and rammed down the bore of the gun, followed by a wad (**17**), the type of shot desired, and another wad. The rope, or 'flexible' rammer (**18**), an especially thick length of rope with a small wooden ramming head at one end and a sponge head at the other, could be used in the restricted space of a gun deck where standard wooden-handled rammers and sponges could not. The worm (**19**) was used during the process of reloading to remove any shreds of the cartridge bag left behind from the previous discharge that might remain in the bore, and which could set off the premature explosion of the next charge if still smouldering. After firing, a member of the gun crew would dip the sheepskin-covered head of the sponge (**20**) in water and insert it down the barrel

in order to extinguish any fragments of cartridge bag or wadding that might ignite the next charge.

D: SWORDSMANSHIP

Part of a seaman's week was devoted to weapons training. These men are practising their skills with swords, for which no standard system of drill existed until the war with France had nearly ended. Having received formal training in the use of edged weapons, some officers assumed the initiative and formulated their own training regimes for the lower ranks. Note the traditional long queue, or pigtail, worn by the man on the left – a common practice and telltale sign of a sailor.

E: RELAXING BELOW DECKS

One officer condemned 'the whole of the shocking, disgraceful transactions of the lower deck [which are] impossible to describe – the dirt, filth, and stench; the disgusting conversation; the indecent beastly conduct and horrible scenes; the blasphemy and swearing; the riots, quarrels and fighting'. While aboard ship men welcomed any opportunity for the company of the opposite sex (**1**), who sometimes descended in their hundreds when a ship docked in port. With gunpowder, tar and other explosives and inflammable materials about, smoking (**2**) was strictly forbidden below decks. Some sailors, oblivious to the extreme danger, ignored the ban, or chose to chew rather than smoke their tobacco. Music assumed an important role in the lives of the ship's company. Here a disabled sailor plays the fiddle (**3**), which he might accompany with a song with a nautical theme to it. 'By such means as this', Leech observed, 'sailors contrive to keep up their spirits amidst constant causes of depression and misery.'

Literacy was extremely rare among ordinary ratings, but a few, armed with a few years' primary education, could put it to limited use in reading and writing letters (**4**). The general absence of any formal education among the lowest ranks accounts for the dearth of memoirs written by the common 'tar'. Gambling (**5**) was forbidden, but many captains, while not openly condoning this popular diversion of the times, turned a blind eye to a practice that they regarded as fairly harmless and, in any event, impossible to suppress altogether. Fighting (**6**), sometimes in anger, sometimes in jest, was a frequent occurrence. Drinking (**7**) was unquestionably the foremost form of recreation for the sailor of Nelson's day. Not only did drunkenness account for the vast majority of floggings, it played a principal part in over half the cases of mutiny, indiscipline and negligence brought before courts martial.

F: BOARDING

With prize money and glory as their chief incentives, British crews were keen to board an enemy vessel and seize it intact. Here the attackers scramble over the gunwales wielding a variety of weapons. The standard sea-service musket with bayonet (**1**) was not easy to manage in the confines of a crowded deck, but it did provide its bearer with three options: to fire it once; to lunge with the bayonet; and to employ the stock as a club. The blunderbuss (**2**) was an effective anti-personnel weapon when loaded with scrap metal and discharged at short range. The scarf tied round the seaman's head kept sweat and blood from obscuring his vision. Heavy and crudely made, yet ideal for combat at sea, the cutlass (**3**) was the classic edged weapon of the age of fighting sail.

Mounting the canvas-covered nettings, a sailor clutches a tomahawk (**4**), or boarding axe, whose short handle suited close-quarter fighting. Literally 'armed to the teeth', another seaman prepares to do battle with a dirk (**5**) clenched in his mouth, a curved sword (**6**) firmly held in his right hand and a brace of pistols (**7**) suspended from a cross-belt slung over his left shoulder, pirate-style. The shipmate on his 'port' side clutches a short pike (**8**), which offered the advantage of jabbing a foe at a distance, yet leaving the attacker vulnerable if he failed to strike his target on the first attempt.

G: TREATING THE WOUNDED

A weary, blood-spattered surgeon (**1**) receives another wounded seaman (**2**), brought to the cockpit suffering from multiple wounds. Loblolly men (**3**), or surgeon's assistants, bore patients down ladders and through hatchways without the aid of stretchers, to the considerable additional discomfort of the stricken sailor. Surgery was a crude, messy and at times gruesome affair, performed in an age of little understanding of the crucial need to keep instruments sterile and hands cleaned between patients. Treatment was largely confined to probing for and extracting shell fragments, musket balls and splinters, if lodged in the head or abdomen, or amputation if an extremity were smashed or likely to go gangrenous if not removed. The surgeon's tray (**4**) contains various instruments including amputating saws and knives. The bottle (**5**) would contain strong spirits as a crude anaesthetic. A brazier (**6**) warms the instruments to lessen the shock of cold steel against exposed flesh, while beside it stands a barrel (**7**) to receive amputated limbs. The surgeon's medicine chest (**8**) contained a variety of (largely ineffective) remedies.

H: PREPARING FOR BATTLE

Following directions issued on the quarterdeck, a seaman (**1**) hoists a series of signal flags to convey a message to other vessels prior to an engagement.

The most famous naval signal of the age, 'England expects that every man will do his duty' (**2**), was raised aboard Nelson's flagship, the *Victory*, before the battle of Trafalgar (21 October 1805) using an ingenious new system introduced five years earlier. Admiral Sir Home Popham's innovation constituted the world's first alphabetic flag system, which employed a numbered dictionary of pre-defined words and phrases. In this case, only 'duty' needed to be spelled out with separate flags to represent each individual letter (bottom row). All the other words could be spelled out with a series of three flags for each.

Seamen (**3**) removing furniture from the captain's cabin to be stowed in the hold during battle. Everything either inessential to the fighting efficiency of the ship or potentially harmful to the crew, including partitions and bulkheads, had to be removed to facilitate the handling of the guns and to minimize the danger of flying splinters.

Middle watch on deck. This scene conveys something of the discomfort experienced by men bracing themselves against cold wind and approaching rain. In inclement weather sailors might wear a pea jacket and a frock (jumper) or obtain limited protection from an oilskin jacket and hat. Conversely, in hot weather, they sometimes had a duck (un-twilled cotton) jacket and frock. (Royal Naval Museum)

INDEX